Derek Jarman

Titles in the series Critical Lives present the work of leading cultural figures of the modern period. Each book explores the life of the artist, writer, philosopher or architect in question and relates it to their major works.

Derek Jarman

Michael Charlesworth

REAKTION BOOKS

Published by Reaktion Books Ltd
33 Great Sutton Street
London EC1V 0DX, UK

www.reaktionbooks.co.uk

First published 2011

Printed and bound in Great Britain
by CPI/Antony Rowe, Chippenham, Wiltshire

British Library Cataloguing in Publication Data
Charlesworth, Michael
    Derek Jarman. – (Critical lives)
    1. Jarman, Derek, 1942-1994.   2. Motion picture producers and
    directors – Great Britain – Biography.   3. Artists – Great Britain –
    Biography.   4. Authors, English – 20th century – Biography.
    5. Set designers – Great Britain – Biography.
    6. Gardeners – Great Britain – Biography.
    I. Title II. Series
    947'.0841'092-DC22

ISBN 978 1 86189 860 9

Contents

Derek Jarman in Robin Noscoe's garden at his house in Canford, 1991.

Preface

Derek Jarman wrote a series of highly readable and fascinating books. They took the form of memoirs, journals and commentaries on the making of films. All gave him the opportunity to use an autobiographical approach, but each work allowed the author's voice to be developed into differing forms, more or less experimental, sometimes modulating between prose and poetry. Although he employed the first person singular, it would be a mistake to regard these works as simple and unproblematical reports from the daily continuing life of Derek Jarman, who was born in 1942 and died in 1994. Like the poets Alexander Pope, W. B. Yeats and many others before him, Jarman engaged in a mythopoeia – a personal mythmaking which kept its eye on a different sense of time (on posterity) and which allowed different emphases about the life and work to emerge in different volumes. Jarman's partner and editor Keith Collins gives a clue to this in his preface to *Kicking the Pricks* (1987):

> Derek extensively re-edited and re-ordered the text, scrubbing out the past, inverting meanings, ruthlessly cutting so that pages were returned bleeding from their red Pentel duels – a process of revision and re-invention that was characteristic in his painting, writing, film editing, and personal history.

Jarman's books are works of literary art rather than straightforward notes. In them he represents to us where his imagination was dwelling at various stages in his life, and obviously the imagination can occupy a somewhat different place from the physical body. Since the imagination is the spring of all creative activity, Jarman offers a wonderful insight to an artist and poet at work. A reader of his books will soon notice that the same incidents are often told in rather different ways. It would be invidious and short-sighted of us to demand that the versions of the story should be identical. The new occasions demanded new emphases. Each context was different. Rather than seeing this as a series of masks hiding the real face of Jarman, we could see them as signs of the manifold nature of personality in modern circumstances. As Jarman himself put it (or rather, as the resonant narrative voice put it) on the soundtrack to his most autobiographical film, *The Garden* (1990): 'I went in search of myself. There were many paths, and many destinations.'

Jarman is famous for his film-making and his place in the history of film-making is assured. Throughout his life he produced paintings and made other works of visual art, including installations and three-dimensional works. This part of his productivity has been much less frequently discussed than his films, despite having given rise to a series of one-man shows between 1961 and 1994, in Europe, the USA and Japan. He designed sets for other people's productions in ballet, opera, film and theatre, and from 1979 made pop promotional films (music videos). Having developed a lifetime of expertise in gardening, Jarman also made an extraordinary garden in a most unlikely place, and lived to see it become nationally famous. This book will aim to tread some of the 'many paths' represented by these activities. Does more than one path lead to the same destination? Do any paths cross each other, or run beside each other for a while? In other words, can the varied activities be conceptually or aesthetically linked?

One path that weaves in and out of Jarman's landscape is that of political activity, which is closely related to his sexuality. The view taken in this book is that he was able to develop political positions out of questions of sexuality and articulate them in ways that became relevant and urgent to a far wider audience than the up to 15 per cent or so of the population who are of a queer orientation. In speaking and writing of gay rights at a time of great controversy about them, Jarman reached an audience far larger than that consisting only of his peers. He did this by relating questions of sexuality to class conflict and governmental questions, and in so doing became a highly successful activist for greater acceptance of homosexuality, because of, rather than despite, his preparedness to engage in controversies during the last eight years of his life. His utterances about class, government, capital and patterns of cultural production, stemming from his own experience more than from an ideological or theoretical position, are also relevant and important to hetero-sexuals, as are his writings on sexuality, its attempted suppression and its free exercise. This was recognized by a large number of people during his lifetime. The ability to reach a wider audience also depended on fame beyond the confines of the film world only, and once the excellence of his garden had been understood by the large, diverse but generally not revolutionary nation of garden-lovers, he was accepted by them for its sake with no regard to whether his sexuality corresponded to theirs or not.

So Jarman the film-maker and Jarman the queer activist have been discussed significantly over the last twenty years or so. Defining him as solely one or the other (or even as both) leaves out a very large amount of his life. The task of a critical biography is to report the life and give as full as possible a critical analysis of the works – in this case works of film, literature, painting, gardening and design. The present state of critical attention to Jarman's engagement in these areas is uneven. There has been in fact very little written about any of the activities except the film-making and the activism. Tony Peake's biography of 1999, a magnificent work of care and detail, will remain unsurpassed as the last word on the facts of Jarman's life for the foreseeable future, but it does not attempt extensive critical analysis of the works. Jarman's own writings offer invaluable views into his imaginative and intellectual life above and beyond the level of facts that Peake establishes. This book takes these bodies of work, together with the Jarman Papers in the archive of the British Film Institute, as its frame of reference from which to derive assistance in characterizing the man and his aesthetic achievements.

It will be hard for this book to do justice to a man who possessed an uncanny ability to 'get you on his side'. For most of his life Derek Jarman was strong, impressive, full of energy and ideas. Without being prompted, people who knew him will state that he was 'charismatic'.[1] However, perhaps not all of that will be lost from this account of his life and works.

It will be a peculiarity of this book after this preface to refer to him as Derek, rather than by his last name. Derek was the name he chose, from among the forenames available to him (Michael Derek Elworthy) and it is impossible to spend any time talking with his old friends without using the name Derek. Calling him Derek also removes his identity from his patronymic, and as we shall see there are good reasons to do this.

1

The View from Dungeness

While retaining his London flat, Derek made Dungeness, the southernmost tip of Kent, his 'place to stand' in 1987. This was the seashore he made famous with his garden. He repeatedly stated that establishing his garden was a more important activity for him than film-making or painting. The garden challenged and absorbed his creativity. It was a continuing process rather than a product, and constituted its own reward without having to be bought and sold or evaluated by critics. 'I'm building this garden now,' he said on BBC Radio in 1990, 'which is my chief joy and delight, as long as I can do that, that's all I really want to do.'[1]

Dungeness forms an exposed point, a sharp promontory. On a sunny day the sea is a deep-water blue, sparkling with sunlight in the wind-blown spray. A stately procession of big ships steams constantly past, heading down the English Channel towards the north Atlantic. Deep-water fish can be caught with rod and line from the steeply sloping shingle bank.

Looking inland, Dungeness forms the southerly apex of a triangle that embraces the high shingle banks and, within and beyond, the grassy levels of the marshes (Denge, Walland and Romney) reaching up to the triangle's northern boundary formed by the low rolling hills between Hythe and Rye. The 150 or so flat square miles embraced in this view fall into two unequal parts: the marshes, green, grassy and rushy; and the Ness, formed from great gently undulating shingle banks, with little to no soil. On

Romney Marsh sheep-farming has traditionally predominated, with increasing arable recently. On the Ness the traditional occupation has been fishing. While the tip of the Ness is washed clean by deep water, in the vast sweeps of bay reaching towards Hythe and Rye great stretches of sand are exposed at low tide.

On the Ness no soil is apparent, but this is no empty landscape. Most of the houses are built of wood. A huge modernist building in three parts, the nuclear power station, stands on the southern shore-line. Pylons lead away from it. The area is served by a steam railway: the Romney, Hythe & Dymchurch, which has a miniature track with rails about a foot apart sitting on dwarf sleepers. Between Dungeness's giant nuclear power station (visible from 25 miles away on the North Downs above Charing on a clear day) and the one-third scale railway, one's sense of proportion reels, and there are no trees, no hedges, no green fields to re-establish the norms. The painter Paul Nash applied the phrase 'seaside Surrealism' to Swanage in Dorset, but the term might suit Dungeness well.

View of Dungeness power station from Jarman's back garden, 2009.

In 1987 Derek moved into a small, four-room, watertight and weatherproof fisherman's house, built of wood in the early twentieth century. He added an extension, a sunroom and bathroom, in 1992. It is one of the beauties of Dungeness that there are no enclosures – no fences, walls or hedges around the houses. If there happen to be no clouds, the sun is with you all day, since there are no trees or hills to obstruct it. Derek's garden therefore lies open to its surroundings, and he had to hit on strategies that worked with the peculiarities of the situation rather than against them (this involved particularly the choice of plants, which not only had to be able to survive, but also had to look as if they belonged). To make the cottage's surroundings seem like a garden he installed a lot of upright posts, thus supplying some of the missing sense of enclosure and working against the relentless horizontality of the landscape while picking up the upright theme from some of its manmade features, most obviously the lighthouses and the pylons. He also made the front garden announce art, introducing geometry

Prospect Cottage and front garden, 1990.

with circular and square patterns in stone, embellished with favourite garden plants. Thus between the cottage and the road a series of circular and quadrilateral patterns rise from the shingle, formed from exceptionally large and long flint pebbles, rounded by the working of the sea and tossed up on the beach. Circles and ellipses of pebbles, placed on end like miniature stone henges, establish the shapes. White and grey stones colour in the patterns set up by the henges, and cushiony tufts of poppies, santolina or lavender, with small herbaceous borders on either side and in front of the cottage windows complete a striking nearly symmetrical arrangement. Plants grow vigorously, as if they find an improbable source of sustenance in the uncompromising shingle. Derek dug trenches beneath the pebbles, filled them with dung and soil, and replaced the pebbles, in order to sustain his plants while not disrupting the remarkable appearance of Dungeness. In summer the patterns of stones are overwhelmed by the flowers, but they are reasserted in winter when the plants die back to lay bare the underlying structure. The pebble henges became famous far in excess of their size.[2]

The back garden is landscape: that is, the gardening arts of plant selection and composing have been used to make the garden seem like the product of nature and time, to form a continuum with the terrain lying around it that is visual and conceptual as well as topographic, looking at least as far down the Ness as the lighthouse (its towering form echoed in miniature by Jarman's upright timbers in the foreground as you look from the house). As the nature writer Roger Deakin saw it, 'Jarman made his garden – but a wild one in a wild way, which would shade off into the wilderness of the beach, into the natural profusion of plants growing there.'[3] To make the garden seem natural, or wild, Derek employed many native plants found growing in the area (for Dungeness, though made of shingle, supports a tenacious flora) and blended the back garden into the wide landscape view that the absence of trees and hills gave him.

Prospect Cottage's back garden and surroundings, 2010. The smoke comes from a Romney, Hythe & Dymchurch Railway train; beyond that is the power station.

He planted circles of gorse, which grows all over Dungeness, valuing the strong green-black foliage and its contrast with the deep bright saturated yellow of the flowers, but also hinting that his was a garden of love via the commonplace saying, quoted in his book *Modern Nature*, that 'kissing's out of season when the gorse is not in flower' (in fact gorse is capable of blooming at any time of the year). Thrift, seakale and horned poppy are other wild plants that he made use of. The result of this twin strategy of making the garden both artful and an extension of the natural world lying around it is a subtle, beautiful garden that seems to concentrate elements of the surrounding territory. And some of those elements are cultural: most of the uprights planted in the garden are relics left over from other purposes, mostly marine. Disused timbers from fishing or driftwood from the beach stand not far from twisted metal rods planted to carry barbed wire as an anti-invasion defence during the Second World War. Old fishing-net floats, oil cans that have spent so much time in the sea before arriving at Dungeness's beach that they seem more like natural than man-made objects, rusting garden tools, all play their part as centrepieces of compositions of forms and colours. While the native plants bring a message of the wild, the domesticated plants, from the old roses and artichokes to the houseleeks and the opium poppies, come with strong cultural associations. 'Consider the world's diversity', Derek had written in his film *Jubilee*, 'and worship it.'

Skies, sunlight, clouds and wind are the chief ingredients of Dungeness, with the shingle a perpetual awkward-to-walk-on matrix and the sea 200 yards from the cottage's front windows a constant changing presence of varying moods. These chief ingredients of being here, together with the plants and the changing colours they give to the Ness, are lyrically described in Derek's journal *Modern Nature* (1991) and the book that appeared just after his death, *Derek Jarman's Garden*. They also feature in his final journal, *Smiling in Slow Motion* (2000), an account of his last three years dying of AIDS. Derek moved to Dungeness shortly after being diagnosed with human immuno-deficiency virus, the virus that opens the door to the illnesses associated with AIDS. The garden helped him to come to terms with his mortality: 'The gardener digs in another time, without past or future, beginning or end . . . As you walk in the garden you pass into this time . . . Around you the landscape lies transfigured. Here is the Amen beyond the prayer.'[4]

The garden also features in his film *The Garden* (1990) which includes footage of Derek working, watering the garden, looking after plants, getting sunburnt. He is also shown sitting in the garden conceiving of and writing the film, *The Garden*, itself, so that the process of creating the film becomes part of the film. This was one way of dramatizing Derek's own conception of and approach to film, where he demanded a cinema that made the film-maker's experience central to the creative effort.[5] What is important for us here is that, as was dramatized in the film, this creative experience grows out of gardening. A related point to make is that garden imagery runs through a high proportion of Derek's films. There are two gardens in *Jubilee* (1978) for example. One belongs to John Dee, Queen Elizabeth I's magician, and the film opens within it, finding a court dwarf feeding titbits to some Great Danes. An imbalance in scale between the dogs and the woman allows us to pretend for a moment that she might be normal size and the dogs as big as horses, and this strikes a light-hearted note that is sustained throughout the film in spite of its bleak themes. Dee's tranquil garden is contrasted with the film's second one, a garden made entirely of plastic by the anti-social ex-soldier Max. The fact that the plastic garden is obviously sterile is indicative of how denatured life has become in the dystopic future imagined in the film.

Gardens recur in *Imagining October* (1984), *The Angelic Conversation* (1985), in Derek's contribution to *Aria* (1987), in *The Last of England* (1987), in *War Requiem* (1989) and in *Blue* (1993) and their significance will be discussed in relation to those films in due course. For the moment it is sufficient to acknowledge that, even before Derek's formation of the garden at Dungeness, gardening was central to his creativity (gardens feature in his paintings and his poetry from the 1960s). One of the points made by no less an authority than Christopher Lloyd, *doyen* of British gardeners and garden writers of the last three decades of the twentieth century, about the garden at Dungeness, is that it was made by a real expert in composition, design and plants, and could not have been created by a novice.

Prospect Cottage is very much in the English garden tradition, showing a love of plants and growing them well as a personal satisfaction. Like all good gardeners, Jarman worked with the natural conditions presented to him by the locale. The fact that he was not put off by being told that gardening at Dungeness was 'impossible', and of there being no protocol or guidance, is also in the English tradition. I feel privileged to have been on the scene when I was, though sad that an acquaintanceship had not the time to become much more than that. Jarman was a man whom I regarded deeply and his garden was a manifestation of great depth and total originality.[6]

Another garden expert who admired Derek's garden and sent him presents of plants was Beth Chatto. What these two experts found was that the harsh conditions of Dungeness had forced adaptations in the native plants' habits of growth and in their colour. So the toadflax and foxgloves, for example, seemed like different plants compared with what Lloyd knew. And Derek's cardoon, open to all the winds that blow at Dungeness, did not need to be staked, as Lloyd's taller cardoon had to be in his Sussex garden, Great Dixter. As Lloyd idiosyncratically expresses it, 'Jarman . . . well understood which plants would like him under these extreme conditions.' Derek understood this because by the time he moved to Dungeness he had a lifetime of experience with plants and composition. Indeed, long before writing and film-making, Derek's earliest creative acts were acts of painting and gardening.

2

Schoolboy and Student

Derek Jarman was born on 31 January 1942, in the middle of a global war. On the night of his birth RAF Bomber Command sent 72 planes to bomb the German-occupied French port of Brest. Five planes failed to return. On this birth day, Britain's evacuation of Malaya was completed, although Singapore had yet to surrender to the Japanese, which happened when Derek was two weeks old. His father, Lance Jarman, a New Zealander, was a Squadron Leader in the RAF, flying bombers, for a lengthy period as a Pathfinder, which meant leading the main bombing echelon to the target and illuminating it by dropping incendiaries and flares. This was a most important and responsible task. Lance Jarman's approach was to ignore the flak.

Lance is remembered in family circles as a very peculiar man. Evidently he had difficulty leaving behind, even after 1945, the violence he had experienced in his war-life. He would beat his children, Derek and Derek's sister Gaye, if they didn't eat their meals. Once on the evening of a dinner-party Derek had earache and began crying. Not wanting his cries from another part of the house to disturb dinner, Lance beat him until he was quiet, and the next day the doctor drained an abscess in Derek's ear. Later Lance beat Derek for using the wrong ('non-U') words, such as 'pardon?' Perhaps this approximated a normal level of domestic violence for the time. However, a different situation, more akin to torture, arose over Derek's food intake when Lance would attempt to force-feed his son (probably about when Derek was three or four years old). We can imagine a grim unequal struggle, chokings, 'screaming and being sick', tears, and a direful apprehension looming around the next mealtime.[1] In light of this it is interesting to see a possibly related incident in one of the sections of Lance's home-movie footage that Derek included in his film *The Last of England* (1987). The sequence shows Derek, at the age of about two, happily running around a garden. His mother sits on a rug nearby, and as Derek approaches and bends down to pick up something from the rug his mother surreptitiously pushes a cup against his lips to try to induce him to drink. This is only a small piece of evidence, but it might suggest that even at this early stage both parents had become obsessively anxious about Derek's eating. The historical context, of course, was one of food rationing, so the spectre of waste was added to the worry about health.

This brings up the question of the part played by Derek's beautiful mother Betts throughout his life and her contribution to the peculiar emotional economy of the Jarman household. Derek seems never to have said a critical or dubious word about her. To her own father she was 'ever-smiling Betty', and she is cast as the peace-maker and the inspirer in Derek's accounts of his upbringing. Nevertheless, she loved and tolerated her husband, who is cast as the bully of the story. Her toleration of Lance somehow made the situation seem acceptable: she loved him, so he must be alright, as Derek put it later.[2] After she became ill with cancer when Derek was eighteen, her illness enforced the appearance of peace in the family, deterring Derek from confronting his father over his feeling of injustice. This silence necessitated by Betts' illness carried on until her death eighteen years later. The idea of the family's strong feelings being sacrificed on the altar of protecting Betts from them is a rather memorable one. Did 'ever-smiling Betty' teach the middle-class goal that everything must have a 'face' of respectability put on it despite the emotional falsification required by that face? Derek wrote later that her smile and charm were perhaps 'the disaster of her time and class'.[3] One other piece of evidence tends to complicate her son's loving account of her: her own brother's characterization was that she was 'bossy and batty'.[4]

The main point of directing attention here to paternal conflict is not to make a point about the adult Derek's apparently completely utilitarian attitude to food (which in any case would have been complicated by years of school meals) but to establish that at a very early age Derek's experience of life included a nasty and lengthy conflict with authoritarian violence, although not, at this stage, a violence visited on him because of his sexuality (that would come later). He took refuge in his grandmother's garden, where, he claimed later, he stood and watched the garden grow.[5] Thinking back to gardens of his childhood, Derek wrote: 'a garden, where poor wayward humanity is capable of being swayed by emotions which make for peace and beauty'.[6] Moments spent in other gardens proved memorable: in Italy when Lance Jarman was posted there in 1946, at the Villa Zuassa on Lake Maggiore, and in the Borghese Gardens in Rome. These were complemented by the parental gift of what became a favourite book, *Beautiful Flowers and How to Grow Them*, the influence of which not only became wholly internalized, but gave rise to conscious decisions in later art and set design for ballet.[7] The family moved around between RAF postings, and Derek took a lot of responsibility for making and maintaining the garden at each. As an adult he also had gardens in pots at the end of his famous room at Bankside, wired later to the rear balcony of his Charing Cross Road flat.

Derek's upbringing was what we used to call upper middle class. The Jarmans were not rich, but money was not necessarily in particularly short supply. There were a few blissful and very memorable months lived in a Jacobean manor house in the west of England. There was foreign travel and living abroad in exotic locations (Italy, Pakistan). Derek was sent away to boarding school.

This introduced him to an entire class and formation in society, and a way of bringing it up, and also gave him the freedom to reject it.

The schools his parents chose for him were in the south-west of England. At eight and a half he became a boarder at his prep school, Hordle House, Hampshire, near the Solent. Perhaps to familiarize him with the region, the family holiday in 1950 was spent in Swanage, some way along the coast. This holiday introduced Derek to a stretch of coast that he came to identify himself with. Swanage stands at the eastern end of a coastline that features three places mentioned in his memoirs or used in his films: Tilly Whim (mentioned at the end of the film *Jubilee*), Dancing Ledge, which gave its name to his first published memoir in 1984, and Winspit, where he filmed parts of *The Angelic Conversation* and *Jubilee*. It is a compelling stretch of coast. Cliffs up to a hundred feet high along the sea's edge are riddled with old quarry workings (giving Dancing Ledge and Tilly Whim their strange names). From the clifftops the land rises steeply to the edge of a plateau a quarter of a mile inland, some 350 feet above sea level. The high, long, south-facing slope is covered with grass, bushes and flowers and is full of butterflies and birds. It amounts to a little world of its own, cut off from the rest of England, entered by no roads and possessing only one house. On a hot summer's day it feels like the Mediterranean. Derek later visited this coast on days out from his school, Canford, and those must have felt like days released from prison: full of ecstatic feelings of freedom.

At Hordle House a traumatic incident when he was nine years old caused Derek to understand that his happiness was the target of attack and brutalization. He was found in bed giggling with another boy. He relates the incident in *Kicking the Pricks* (1987):

My crime was prosecuted by the headmaster with more violence than any other misdemeanour in the school . . . We were beaten, hauled up in front of the whole school, threatened with expulsion, and the terrible consequences our actions would have on our families if they were revealed. This public exposure gave me a terrible shock and opened wounds that will never heal.[8]

His behaviour and his performance in school became traumatized: 'I was set apart'. His recounting of this incident, in a section entitled 'Child Abuse', is printed on a page opposite a photograph of himself at his most innocent: picking flowers with his sister and his mother. This placing alone perhaps conveys some of the bitterness Derek felt at how he had been treated. In fact he returned to the incident repeatedly, in *Dancing Ledge* (1984), *Kicking the Pricks*, *Modern Nature* (1991) and *At Your Own Risk* (1992).

One of the best things about Hordle School was the allocation to the boys of plots in a walled garden for them to make their own gardens. While other boys grew vegetables, Derek already showed an aptitude for growing flowers, a skill that gave him an early experience of prize winning. The garden at Hordle amounted to a compensation for the spartan regime and various traumas – boxing classes, for example, as well as the more serious incidents – that Derek lived through there.

After several years struggling with stigma, feelings of isolation and grim school food, with mischievous schoolboy humour as his main defence, in alliance with friendships that the boys negotiated, Derek went as a boarder to one of the lesser public schools, Canford, just over the county boundary in Dorset. Putting Derek through public school was a key part of Lance Jarman's project to bring Derek up as an English gentleman. Born and brought up in New Zealand, Lance had come to Britain and worked his way up in the RAF from the early 1930s. He despised the British establishment but also wanted to buy into it. Public school gave Derek first-hand experience of class at work, especially the formation of class-consciousness in the young or new members of that class. In it he experienced the system that destroyed Britain. And by putting him through this class system his education gave him the freedom to reject it: 'the terrorists in *The Last of England* are the establishment', he wrote later.[9]

Derek described Canford as a home of 'muscular Christianity'. It is interesting to compare his accounts of his time at Canford with John Le Carré's very similar condemnations of another west country public school that he had attended some ten years earlier, Sherborne.[10] The schools are condemned for strongly parallel reasons: the schools were out of touch spiritually and politically; the ethos of sentimentality towards the schools' own past and system (for example, the 'House' system of built-in rivalries, which helped to martyr Derek when his House's annual winning of the Art Cup, in which he participated, led to bullying from his own House's athletes, who failed to win the rugby cup) matched a sentimentality towards Britain's own past that the schools perpetuated. Class- and race-hatreds were fostered. Derek wrote later 'I hate the voice of my kind. I know who they are, brain-washed in mediocre public schools, brought up to rule over the oiks and wogs.'[11] Both authors also hated the muscular Christianity promoted and policed by the masters, the adults' turning of blind eyes to the endemic bullying that went on among the boys, and the false value systems perpetuated by the schools. Then there was the entirely strange atmosphere created by removing hundreds of boys from the company of the opposite sex and requiring them to live at very close quarters to each other. For heterosexual boys this presented a lot of problems, in some cases serious and even occasionally leading to pathological behaviour. For homosexual boys a different set of problems presented themselves, different but no less serious. Having to live with a load of heterosexuals driven to the edge of pathological behaviour by their deprivation, for a start.

Another traumatic violent incident happened to Derek at Canford, in which his sexuality was centrally involved. There are signs that he was singled out or alienated at the school. He was rumoured to be very well-endowed physically, which would thus make him an object (I use the word deliberately) of interest. One of his nicknames was 'Wog' since he was relatively dark-skinned, so much so in fact that he began to speculate about having Maori blood and, through his grandmother Rueben, Jewish blood, and, since his mother's family had come from India during the Empire, Indian blood. In the incident in question he became the victim of intense psycho-sexual violence committed against him by a group of boys. This incident he never mentioned in print. In conversation with his friend Ron Wright he used the word 'rape' about it, but the rape was of such a kind that Derek's was the only body exposed and humiliated: it seems rather akin to types of torture against prisoners perpetrated in more recent years by elements of the U.S. army in Abu Ghraib prison in Iraq.[12] The public removal from him, in the most traumatic circumstances, by violence and against his will, of control over his sexuality, was an outrage of the most psychologically wounding kind.

Derek later told Keith Collins that the years at Canford had been 'the most unhappy' years of his life.[13] He was saved from the added humiliation of academic failure by his own talents, recognized by two of the masters. Andrew Davis, the English master, particularly praised an essay Derek wrote on Cleopatra as Isis (I haven't read the essay, but the subject suggests that even at this stage Derek's literary interests were capable of branching out in an occult direction). This gave Derek confidence and a redoubled enthusiasm for the subject which together helped him to do well. There was a good reason why, years later, Derek criticized Pink Floyd's song 'Another Brick in the Wall (Part II)' – 'we don't need no education . . . we don't need no thought control' – on the grounds that teachers might just be giving the pupils the tools they need to reject and fight the system.[14] The other master who understood Derek's abilities was the art master, Robin Noscoe, whose 'Art Hut' represented a counter-order to that of the larger school, a place for the budding artists to stand, its ethics emblazoned above the windows in a quotation from Eric Gill:

AN ARTIST IS NOT A SPECIAL KIND OF MAN
BUT EVERY MAN IS A SPECIAL KIND OF ARTIST[15]

As Tony Peake emphasizes, Noscoe became the most profound artistic influence on Derek and, in 1990, when Clare Paterson, the producer of the BBC series *Building Sights*, asked Derek to contribute a nine-minute film about his favourite building, he chose Robin Noscoe's house (designed by Noscoe himself and worked on by some of the boys). The segment of the series that went out the week before Derek's film was broadcast saw Alice Rawsthorne, design correspondent of the *Financial Times*, giving essentially an efficient academic lecture on St Olave's House, a Thames-side art deco office and warehouse on the South Bank in London. The week after Derek's film Alan Bennett talked about a shopping arcade in Leeds, delivering a thimbleful (nine minutes) of social history with humour and dead-pan enthusiasm, mixing it up with personal reminiscences in Bennett's inimitable style. This segment on the County Arcade was directed expertly by David Hinton.

So Derek's film, directed by Keith Collins, was broadcast between these two, and has a hand-made quality. Noscoe's Garden House dates from 1959 (when Derek was in the sixth form). Derek claims it echoes many 1950s buildings, such as Le Corbusier's Notre Dame du Haut in Ronchamp. He likes the personal aspect of it, the wit and charm, and the way the house reflects its owner, 'unfinished, full of the clutter of a lifetime'. Much of the film simply shows us things and details rather than the overall view. The house has a bricolaged aspect. Features were by choice or of necessity recycled from other places, such as the medieval door from Poole, and there are found objects, such as fossils and wheel hubs. Plenty of paintings by Noscoe's pupils are in the house, including one painted by Derek at the Slade School of Art in 1963 when 'we thought painting important then'. In Noscoe's study is the door from a demolition site that Derek carved and painted with a text from the *Canterbury Tales*. Noscoe himself made most of the furniture.

If Noscoe's Art Hut saved Derek's sanity at school, or at least his emotional life, it must have been a thrill to help the master make his house. The house and the way it was lived in must have represented something of an ideal for Derek. The programme is a celebration of the partly hand-made house less for itself than as a container for a life well lived, reflecting Noscoe's personal qualities, the humour, the compassion for pupils, the practical capability and ingenuity. (A Wyndham Lewis-influenced self-portrait that Derek painted at Canford School around this time hung over Derek's workbench in the painting room at Dungeness in the last years of his life.)

So far as university was concerned, Lance Jarman insisted that his son should get an academic rather than an art degree, but eventually an agreement was worked out whereby he would pay to put Derek through university twice – first to gain an academic degree, and after that as an art student. Andrew Davis strongly supported this arrangement, so in 1960 Derek went to King's College, London, to read for a general BA (in his case English, Art History and History constituted his courses of study) and afterwards (1963–7) he was an undergraduate art student at the Slade School of Art, choosing to specialize in theatre design. The result was that he was better educated, with a real understanding of literature and history, than would otherwise have been the case, and in this respect owed a big debt of gratitude to his father.

In 1961 Derek entered the *Daily Express* / University of London Union art competition and, jointly with another student, won first prize in the amateur category. The amount was £20, about two and a half weeks' wages for a labourer at the time. His prize-winning painting, *We Wait*, showing a queue of people under a streetlamp, resembles something from the Soviet avant-garde of the 1920s, the rounded faceless doll-like forms of the figures supporting finely worked-out colour relationships. The professional category was won by 24-year-old David Hockney with a painting entitled *The Most Beautiful Boy in the World*. Hockney was five years older than Derek and had already had to make some serious decisions, such as declaring conscientious objection during his National Service. Given that Derek was being forced to wait before going to art school, and was waiting for the release of his sexuality, both waits determined by the conservatism of his upbringing, it is very tempting to read the subject-matter emblematically. Perhaps on the basis of his prize, Derek enjoyed a proper one-man exhibition in the public library of his (and his parents, since he lived at home) local town, Watford.

More sexual violence happened, however. In the summer of 1961 Derek hitch-hiked with some friends to Crete. Separated from his friends on the way back, he accepted a lift in Switzerland from a 'tough-looking middle-aged man' who drove off the road among some trees, tried to kiss Derek, unzipped his own trousers, and attempted to force Derek to fellate him. There was a struggle, tears and a lengthy ordeal of extrication.[16] At the age of nineteen, having been brutally attacked without provocation by his father, by the authority figures at Hordle School, by a gang of other boys at Canford and by a rapist in Switzerland, three of these attacks directly targeted at his sexuality, Derek had every reason to feel, beneath his charming exterior, extremely angry.

While at King's, Derek took a course (through Birkbeck) with the architectural historian Nikolaus Pevsner, an experience he remembered joyfully all his life. An English tutor, Eric Mottram, introduced him to the work of the Beats, a group of jazz-influenced, drug-influenced u.s. writers including William Burroughs, Jack Kerouac and Allen Ginsberg, and this remained another lifelong influence. When he got to the Slade at last in 1963, Derek at first felt slightly behind, having to catch up to the expectations of an academic course of practice, and having to expose his art to more daunting criticism than had ever been the case before. He also found that he couldn't draw as well as other people.[17]

A painting from Derek's student days is reproduced here. It is untitled, so purely for the convenience of this book I label it *Painting A*. The paint is mainly white, and has a fluidity that De Kooning would have liked. A green square frames the centre, within the overall square of the painting, and focuses attention on the denser array of colours within. Yellows and a very pale green help to accumulate hues that already exist in the area outside the green square and relay them in more intense and concentrated form. The

Painting A, *c.* 1960–65, oil on canvas.

yellow is applied with a characteristic rapid-fire lower left to upper right stroke that Derek also used in his late Dungeness landscape series. Only a student work, perhaps, but it is a beautiful painting and one that has real presence in the room in which it hangs.

The liberation of Derek's sexuality finally began in 1964, under the warm influence of a Canadian, Ron Wright, who initiated sexual contact between them in London. They hitch-hiked to Italy in the spring and Wright acted as host to Derek on part of his trip to North America in the summer of that year. Wright's sexual interest did not last. He found Derek 'remote physically and very rigid . . . so stiff in his body, almost frozen solid'.[18] What contributing reasons might there have been for this rigidity? The thaw in a life of repression doesn't often come all at once. However much he wanted to, it might have been difficult for Derek to engage in acts that the state classed as criminal and therefore immoral and that his father and mother would be aghast at. Writing later about how Caravaggio, 'growing up with the conventions that surrounded him' probably became bisexual at first, Derek continued, 'Later you hack them away, but the strictures of Church and society leave a cancer, a lingering doubt.'[19] The shift here into the present tense and the word 'you' employed to stand for 'one' or 'one like me' – the generalized subject – surely tell us about Derek's own experience of the internalization of repression. And given that his sexuality had also been wounded by violent attacks, the history of traumatic beatings and encounters might well have been involved in the rigidity that Wright found. The trip to North America helped: Derek visited San Francisco and Monterey and bought (in Calgary he says) his own copies of Allen Ginsberg's poetry and William S. Burroughs's *The Naked Lunch*. He valued the cultural example that Ginsberg's work offered of outspokeness on homosexuality and the political problems of the post-war period very greatly. There was no British equivalent. A chaos of casual sex in New York on the way home also doubtless helped loosen him up. And in London,

Michael Harth became a very supportive friend, introducing Derek to the delights of cruising for sex on Hampstead Heath, which became a lifelong pleasure. 'Sex on the Heath is an idyll pre-fall', Derek wrote in 1989. 'Did Adam masturbate . . .? All the Cains and Abels you could wish for are out on a hot night, the may blossom scents the night air and the bushes glimmer like a phosphorescent counterpane in the indigo sky.' Hampstead Heath by night is a place of freedom, a 'sweet' illusion of equality, 'exciting and joyous', combining queer life with the pleasures of the natural world through stimulus to the senses: silence, cool air, the moon and stars, trees. It is a refuge in which 'the world seems a better place'.[20] So Derek's liberation gathered momentum, even before 1967 saw the long-awaited Parliamentary decriminalization of homosexual acts by consenting men over the age of 21. An era of attempted suppression, enforcement, shame, entrapping and legalized persecution was beginning to end.

The experience of repression, and the struggle out of it, remained as a crucially important experience for Derek, informing small things as well as large. When the time came, as *At Your Own Risk* shows, memory of repression also informed Derek's activism around HIV/AIDS and the skill with which he was able to wage that campaign as well as his refusal to compromise.

At the Slade the course on film started by William Coldstream, the head of the Slade and a founder of the Euston Road School, in 1960, which by Derek's time was taught by the film-maker Thorold Dickinson, introduced Derek to the work of Eisenstein, Carl Dreyer, Jean Renoir, Max Ophuls and Humphrey Jennings. Film was thus introduced within the context of artistic practice, not primarily as a commercial practice. There were visits by film-makers who talked about their work. Derek had already found for himself the work of Fellini, Pasolini, Brakhage, Cocteau and Genet. As yet, though, he didn't think anything of it as a personal possibility. Questions of design were concentrated in another way by the last two years of

Derek's course, when he specialized in theatre design, a component taught by Peter Snow and Nicholas Georgiadis. This will have taught Derek the ins and outs of the ways in which theatrical performance (including ballet and opera as well as plays) amounts to an inherently symbolic form of art. His time as a student ended in 1967 on high notes of success. He had two large paintings exhibited in the 'Young Contemporaries' exhibition at the Tate Gallery on Millbank, a competition open to students at the major London art schools: *Cool Waters* used a real tap and a real towel rail attached to the front of the clear-edged painting, while *Landscape with Various Devices* incorporated an attached pyramid of real sponges and circles of textured material. The latter painting became one of ten winners of the Peter Stuyvesant Foundation Prize for Landscape.

3

Designing for Others, Painting, Super-8

Derek left the Slade with a taste for designs that were modernist, abstract and symbolic. His student design for Ben Jonson's play about a miser, *Volpone*, placed the miser's bed on top of a heap of treasure; his design for Sartre's *Huis Clos* featured an all-crimson set with three armchairs: one green, one black and one blue; and his set for *Orpheus*, seemingly more seminal than the others, given how much he talked and wrote about it afterwards, based the gates of hell on the Brooklyn Bridge, while framing the hell-mouth with a bevy of blown-up photographs of male nudes, and a giant plait of hair hanging like a bell-pull.[1] The next few years gave him important opportunities to test how his designs would work in the world outside the Slade. He entered a chaotic period of wild successes, of deep glooms caused by fiascos, of connections made, some not maintained, of feeling his way through the problems and pleasures of designing for others.

The work of four young British designers was chosen by the British Council for exhibition in the Paris 'Biennale des Jeunes Artistes' of 1967, and Derek was one of them. He exhibited a very striking pair of legs (the centrepiece of another student design, for Prokofiev's ballet *The Prodigal Son*). The critic Guy Brett wrote a favourable review of Derek's contribution in *The Times* ('perhaps the best thing in its section'). Nigel Gosling, critic for the *Observer* and friend of Nikos Georgiadis of the Slade's theatre room, read Brett's review. Gosling had already noticed Derek's painting

Model design for the gates of hell from the opera *Orpheus*, 1967.

Landscape with Marble Mountain, which was shown in the 'Open Hundred' exhibition in Edinburgh, and had also seen his work in the second Lisson Gallery exhibition. Gosling also worked as his paper's ballet critic under a pseudonym, and when Sir Frederick Ashton, choreographer for the Royal Ballet, made it known that he was looking (at somewhat short notice) for a designer, Gosling recommended that he look seriously at Derek Jarman. Ashton's need arose from the Royal Ballet having agreed to fill 'an unexpected gap in the programme of the Royal Opera House'.[2] Ashton recommended Derek, and his recommendation was considered by the design sub-committee of the Royal Opera House, on which William Coldstream (of the Slade) sat.

The upshot was that Derek started his design career at the top, designing *Jazz Calendar* for the Royal Ballet (performed in January 1968). There was a joke at the time that Derek slept with eminent theatre 'queens' to get to the top, and this has been related by subsequent writers. Lest it should be taken seriously, the trail of recommendation recounted above shows that the merit of his other work set in place a sequence that led to this opportunity. It was a brilliant triumph for Derek: the entire ballet was well received by the press, and his design work was singled out for particularly favourable reviews by, among others, the *Times Educational Supplement*. Jazz music suited his taste for abstraction. The set was spare: a pyramid of plastic spheres, giant numbers painted in camouflage and stripes, a ruddy background, a Miró-like form suspended above. The scene for 'Wednesday' was lit with blue light, projected low, so the dancers' shadows loomed giant alongside the now-blue pyramid. Derek's costumes were particularly successful, playing on black and white, on camouflage, on brilliance and shadow, and on the theme of one dancer appearing to melt into another when they embrace, as in one *pas de deux* each dancer wore one half blue, one half red.

Set design for 'Wednesday' in the ballet *Jazz Calendar*, 1967.

The year 1967 had been an outstanding one, especially since his painting *Landscape with a Blue Pool* had been bought by the Arts Council. After January, 1968 turned into something of a disaster. For the Ballet Rambert Derek designed costumes for the Romanian choreographer Steve Popescu's ballet *Throughway*, which was performed in March. On the second night Popescu committed suicide. He had been unhappy with various aspects of the production, including the 'grotesquerie' (Tony Peake's apt word[3]) of Derek's costumes, but to say that this was the cause of his suicide would be simplistic. Nevertheless, Derek was of course shaken by this experience. The performances ended immediately.

Soon afterwards John Gielgud wrote to Derek inviting him to design the opera *Don Giovanni* for the capital's Sadler's Wells Opera Company (later the English National Opera). So in opera design Derek also started at the top, in the sense of a big production in the metropolis for a very important company. The production inaugurated the opera company's move to the Coliseum in the West End, which was being converted from a cinema, so the months leading up to the production were fraught with building works and attendant difficulty. The production was almost universally disliked by the critics, and both the *Evening Standard* and the *Sunday Times* vilified Derek's designs. These were abstracted and modernist versions of garden scenes and architectural spaces, and perhaps one reason for their lack of success came from having a foot in two camps: they were neither the complete abstractions of *Jazz Calendar*, nor the cosy, comfortable eighteenth-century settings that an audience for Mozart might have expected. The garden scene features a backcloth painted with stylized topiary cones, setting up a crude idea of perspective leading to distant pillars and architectural shapes vaguely reminiscent of a Palladian church, but the audience (and the performers) are psychologically excluded from whatever austere delights it promises by an obtrusive cage-like grid or mesh of rectangles which extended right across the stage in front of it. The opening day of the production in August brought baleful and gloomy news from outside. Newspaper placards read 'Russian Tanks Go In'[4] as Czechoslovakia was invaded by the Soviet Union, the Prague Spring came to an end, and the Czech premier, Alexander Dubček, disappeared. Gielgud's production drew awful reviews.

It was perhaps experiences such as this that led Derek to spend very little time crying over spilt milk, and left him eager to move on to the next promising thing.[5] In 1968 he moved his studio (and in 1969 his dwelling) into an L-shaped room in an old warehouse in Upper Ground, on the south bank of the River Thames in central London. Derek became part of a group of people pioneering living in lofts in warehouses. In his case there were three such dwellings, as in turn they became classified for demolition or luxury redevelopment: Upper Ground gave way to Bankside (1970–72) and then Butler's Wharf (1973–9). It was Bankside that became touted as 'the most beautiful room in London', and where, prompted by a suggestion from an architect friend, Dugald Campbell, Derek solved the problem of keeping warm.[6] A small greenhouse bought at a garden centre, erected within the large warehouse room and used as a bedroom, provided a brilliant solution to the problem of the cold in the unheatable, uninsulated attic room. It also provides a striking image, perpetuating the garden imagery that pervades his life and works, and suggesting that Derek was an ingredient or even a product of gardening, to supplement his interest as a gardener. He was both the garden and the gardener.

In contrast to the ultimately disastrous excitements of the previous year, 1969 was relatively quiet in design terms. Derek was designer for the play *Poet of the Anemones* by Peter Tegel at the Theatre Upstairs at the Royal Court, which saw the first appearance of a cape, which became a feature of Derek's art for a while. In this case the cape was transparent, with dollar bills incorporated into it. In the same year he had a one-man exhibition at the Lisson Gallery, which was appreciatively written up in the fashion magazine *Queen*.

This is probably the point to consider the question of what happened to Derek's painting in the years 1969–80. He stated in *Dancing Ledge* that designing for others, especially in film (which we will examine in a moment) squeezed painting out: time and concentration were simply not available as lavishly as they were up until the end of 1969. This may well have been the case, but one or two other factors must be noticed as well.

The character of Derek's paintings had changed. By the late 1960s and the early 1970s there was none of the exuberant enjoyment of the fluidity of paint that we saw in *Painting A*. The works were almost all landscapes, and they had become colder, more distant, eventually smaller (after the Slade years), more dominated by one colour, often more geometrical, often flatter, or only schematically and minimally spatial, and painted in a hard-edged manner. Some of the smaller of these works are very beautiful.[7] The 'Avebury' series from 1971–2 shows objects that resemble the standing stones of the prehistoric Avebury circle planted in wholly abstract settings that consist of horizontal lines crossed by a minimal number of uprights. Some idea of space is created from the intersection of horizontal and vertical forms, but there is no idea of surface or setting. Very few of these landscapes are populated (and then only with distant, schematic figures) and none are remotely pictur-esque. The paint is applied very thinly, with no visible brushmarks. Distant rocks and cliffs are represented by an interesting collaged element: black and white photographs of marble surfaces are cut up, backed on yellow paper so that a narrow border surrounds the 'rocks' and fixed to the right place on the canvas. Beauty might be present, but a feeling of human emptiness pervades, and a very minimal structure. There is a feeling of extreme rational control, as if everything more exuberant has been sacrificed to cerebral command and intellectual games to do with finding a minimal representation of landscape. The results, however, contain a certain satisfaction and convey a certain pleasure.

From Derek's later writings about his painting within its context of other people's art, a fourfold pattern emerges. First, there is a sense of belatedness. He would have preferred to have gone to art school at the age of eighteen, and not have had to wait until he was 21. And there was always the figure of David Hockney in front of him: older, the pioneer, so much so that Derek writes that he didn't want to be a 'follower' of Hockney (which he gives as a reason for not making painting his primary career focus).[8] Patrick Procktor, too, looms, though never as the outright rival that Hockney becomes, perhaps because Derek's personal relationship with Procktor was warmer. Second, Derek's specialization in theatre design could give the impression that painting was a secondary concern. So do utterances like this from *Dancing Ledge*, in which he talks about how design work for Ken Russell's films squeezed painting out: 'Painting was the major victim: I continued it over the next ten years very sporadically. After the intense pressure under which a film is made, it seemed undemanding – and the isolation in which it is pursued, enervating.'[9]

He writes that he hated 'the struggle' (with painting) and wanted quick results, as if the process of painting didn't intrigue him.[10] The upshot of such an impression is that no matter how brilliant Derek's painting is, many people, encouraged even by his own statements, could take the view that it was of secondary importance to him and therefore must be to them too. A third factor is the question of pursuing painting in isolation, which Derek refers to repeatedly in his writings. What does this mean? Isolation isn't inevitable, as the nineteenth-century studios, the examples of the Pre-Raphaelites, the Impressionists, of Picasso and Braque make clear. Perhaps we should relate this 'isolation' to the shyness and solitariness that Derek talks of living through during his twenties. He wrote later that he thought his generosity with money at this time represented 'distress signals' (masking loneliness and the need for love).[11] But the solitariness could easily be related to the intense competitiveness that Derek felt all his life. He always wanted to win, and not be second (or worse). In painting Derek was isolated in another sense, too, having rejected Pop Art. He couldn't do a Derek Boshier, and dye his hair blonde (also like Hockney) and go to the USA (also like Hockney) making Pop Art. And this is part of a fourth element in the pattern, a more general sense of belatedness. While he was there the Slade closed its antique room. 'Five centuries of the European love-affair with antiquity was quietly labelled "obsolete" by the Slade, its last guardians . . . an apocalypse had overtaken the old dream.'[12] The new dream was the dream of Pop Art. Derek had a keen regard for the past in general and was distressed by wholesale discardings of it whether in painting or architecture. The curtain design in Derek's set of proposals for *Orpheus* shows a desolate landscape of fragments of classical statuary. He would have liked to have been able to participate wholeheartedly in the older obsolescent love-affair. Some indication that he would have been very good at it comes from his painting from 1965, *From Poussin's Inspiration of a Poet*, which has a fluent lyricism in the drawing of the three figures that is very affecting. But it was not to be, at least not in the medium of painting. That his gates of hell designs for *Orpheus* were based on the Brooklyn Bridge was a device that Derek later interpreted as a subconscious comment on 'American Popism', while 'the Elysian Fields . . . are strewn with the perfect fragments of the classical world we are casually discarding'.[13] It was not possible to pursue the old dream in the medium of painting, perhaps. But a different medium awaited in the first few days of the new decade.

The fourfold pattern above is a pattern of extrinsic and contextual factors. The case does not rest on the innate or inherent quality of Derek's paintings, which is variable, like any artist's. He was capable of producing unconvincing works but his best paintings are beautiful, memorable, truly striking, rooted in the circumstances of their making yet far transcending them in effect.

Curtain design for *Orpheus*, 1967.

It is not, in other words, in any sense an argument about quality.
It is the frame for a possible explanation of why Derek seemed to
set his painting on one side, and why many other people since have
thought that they were following him in assuming that it was of less
importance to him than film, or design, or writing, or gardening.
Yet despite his apparently disarming comments, he continued
to have exhibitions in England and on the Continent, in North
America and the Far East until the end of his life. Painting was
not unimportant to him at all.

A small, entirely disinterested and spontaneous act of kindness
on Derek's part changed his entire life, by setting him on the path
of film. For the Christmas of 1969 and the new year's celebrations
he had been in Paris. He was sitting in the train at the Gare du
Nord at the beginning of the journey home. In that era the boat
trains were notoriously crowded, and when he saw a young woman
walking up the platform with two heavy suitcases, judging from

her clothes and her long hair that she was English, he called out of the window to her that there was a spare seat in his compartment. She turned out to be Janet Deuter, who taught at Hornsey Art College and was a friend of the film director Ken Russell. She told Derek that Russell was just starting a new project and that she'd tell him about Derek. Two days later Ken Russell was in the L-shaped room at Upper Ground looking at Derek's records of design work, on the basis of which he offered him the job of designing what became the most controversial and gruelling British film of the period, *The Devils*. Work on the film took up the whole of 1970. It involved designing an enormous set to represent the French town of Loudun in 1634. Given the enormity of the enterprise, the fact that he had never worked in the film industry before in any capacity, and the notoriously bumptious nature of the director, it is a tribute to Derek's spirit that he didn't quail before the challenge. Instead all voices agree that what he did was a triumph. He had extremely skilled and competent support from the art director, George Lack, and the support of friendship from the film's sculptor, Christopher Hobbs, who from this time became a long-term collaborator and close friend.

Drawing on his understanding of architecture, his liking of the Gothic, and with some respect for the renaissance Ideal City paintings, Derek created Loudun as an ideal town that could be understood from its appearance as historical and yet was also modernist in its feeling. *The Devils* is about religion, particularly about how, as Lucretius had put it in *De rerum natura*, 'Tantum Religio potuit suadere malorum' (How greatly religion can sway us towards evil). The story, derived from historical events relayed via Aldous Huxley's book *The Devils of Loudun* (1952), concerns a case of 'demonic possession' among the nuns of the town, the torture of one of them and the consequent brutal torturing and burning alive of the local priest, Urbain Grandier, all of which is filmed most graphically by Russell. What Derek's set does is render the audience unable to picture these hideous events in some picturesque late medieval or now-forgotten early modern past. In other words, the cruelty and inhumanity cannot be easily assimilated to a remote period that we can feel we have now left behind. The point of Huxley's book is that devastating religious bigotry can erupt in any period when religious authorities are given too much power by the state. But there was still more to Derek's designs. Looking back on them from 1984, the *Times* critic wrote that '*The Devils* in particular amazes at a distance of thirteen years by its unblinking use of Post Modern settings at a time when the architectural movement had hardly even begun to define itself.'[14]

All accounts agree that Huxley's sentence comparing the 'exorcism' of an unfortunate nun to 'a rape in a public lavatory' set the emotional, and to some extent the visual, tone for the director and his designer. It also provided an idea for the music, according to Peter Maxwell-Davies, the composer for the film.[15] Derek's cold white sets, antiseptic settings that make lunacy and crime all the more visible, produce the feeling powerfully.

Drawing for the set of Ken Russell's *The Devils* (1970).

An eye-witness gives a brief but invaluable glimpse of how Derek worked with Ken Russell during this period:

> Prue presses letters into Ken's hands, which are signed, while he goes on discussing ideas with Jarman, a calm, colourful gypsy-like young man whose ear-rings, half-boots and embroidered jacket do not detract from an air of studious absorption . . . Russell supplies the motive force, the key structure, and draws on Jarman's visual flair to fill in the spaces. Not afraid to say 'That's wrong' or 'You've done that before', Derek acts as a brake and anchor on Ken's ballooning imagination.[16]

Russell described Derek as a 'bohemian' and his judgement has been echoed, and therefore reinforced, by others. What does this mean? The feature of a bohemian is presumably that he or she is not particularly excited by material success, and therefore cannot be lured and hired by the promise of it. In *Dancing Ledge* Derek tells us how, in the 1960s, he 'mistrusted success' in himself and others (and he means material, rather than artistic success).[17] Instead 'art is the key', and 'art' means taking a particular approach to life.[18] From Derek's writings we receive the strong impression that perfection is only possible in our dreams, that is, in the life of the imagination, and this would probably also extend to perfect happiness. Derek was also prepared to give away his paintings rather than hoard them up for the conversion of artistic excellence to monetary capital through exhibitions, dealers and sales, and to do that is an open, human and bohemian form of behaviour. Some of this bohemianism is perhaps related to the conviction stated later in *Dancing Ledge* that art is theft: that artists steal everyday creativity that the entire world should share.[19] 'Art is theft: the Kine and the Lyre', he wrote again later.[20] This cryptic note refers to the myth of Hermes, inventor of musical instruments and therefore the lyric tradition. Hermes, representing creativity, invented the lyre, but gave it to the Olympian Apollo after his theft of Apollo's cattle.

A rather different idea of creativity motivated another of Russell's films, which Derek also designed, *Savage Messiah* (1972). This film was based on the life of the French sculptor Henri Gaudier, who was killed on the Western Front in 1915 at the age of 23. Apart from two brief Vorticist settings, the design had to be entirely naturalistic, and involved the designer harmonizing locations into the period, and creating period settings in the studio. The film was made on a very low budget with Russell's own money, and did badly at the box office and received poor critical reception when it was released. It contains a lot of ranting and shouting (in fact the director encourages the actors do little else but shout and rant) and represents a completely ludicrous and unreal idea of what art and creativity might be. There is a complete discontinuity between the painstakingly naturalistic sets and the farrago of unreal attitudes and posturings about being creative that the film stages. No doubt Derek learned from this experience – that he could spend his whole life making a living by designing for others and, at the end, have nothing of his own to show for it. Yet money had to be earned, and Derek liked working with the adventurous and irrepressible Russell, so in the spring of 1973 he spent some weeks in Rome working on the director's *Gargantua* before the project fell apart. An unexpected bonus of this was that in Rome he met a new lover, the small, thin, energetic and feminine Gerard Incandela, who came back to London with him in May.

In September 1973 Derek worked for London Festival Ballet's *Silver Apples of the Moon*, only to find 'the best design work I've ever done' banned, along with the rest of the ballet, by the company's director over the issue of the flesh-coloured tights that were worn by the dancers. The production had been planned for the Coliseum.

There were two performances, in Oxford, where, the designer tells us, his set design was greeted by 'spontaneous applause'.[21] The design featured a spectacular effect of light. In the meantime, a series of fires broke out in the warehouses of London's docklands. 'The first to go was the beautiful regency building that John Betjeman had listed after I showed it to him last year.'[22] The rumour at the time was that they had been burned down by property developers eager to get their hands on the riverside land. Derek had had to move out of his beautiful room in Bankside after two brief years, and in 1973 leased part of a warehouse at Butler's Wharf. The fires also came close to this building one night. The last light that had shone in his home at Bankside had come from a film projector. Derek and a group of friends had watched *A Midsummer Night's Dream* and his childhood favourite, *The Wizard of Oz*, and then crept out in the dark without turning the house lights back on. The gloom of aborted projects and the encroaching activities of property developers would have been less easy to bear had it not been for Incandela's presence and for the fact that Derek had started to make his own films in a way very different to Russell's: on a hand-held 8-mm camera (the very first film, *Electric Fairy*, recently rediscovered after being thought lost, was made with the help of Malcolm Leigh on 16 mm[23]). The 8-mm camera excited his creativity and his feelings.

The Super-8 camera was small, light, easy to load and unload, and easy to operate. It came with a built-in light metre, and you could film at various speeds. Derek borrowed his first in 1972 from a visiting guest from America. He acquired his own and started to make short films with it. Tinkering with its materiality and exploring its technical possibilities, he discovered an extraordinary feeling of freedom: 'You don't know what you have to say until you've said it. You can dream of lands far distant.'[24] Quite different from the isolation he had felt when painting, his new hand-held film-making necessitated the cooperation of friends, with Duggie

Fields, Christopher Hobbs, Kevin Whitney, Luciana Martinez and Incandela there from the very beginning. Early subjects were these friends, a walk to the stone circle of Avebury, Egypt, fire, alchemy and the dance of death (in *Death Dance*, 1973). Derek began to conceive of film as a form of alchemy: the union of light and matter, light acting directly to effect change in matter.

Garden of Luxor (1972) exemplifies the simplicity of means by which Derek achieved dream-like effects in these early films. Two postcards – of the Pyramids and of a garden in Luxor – form the basis of this film. One was filmed, then projected onto a postcard of the other scene. The result was re-filmed, using filters to make it sometimes red, sometimes blue. This was then projected onto people standing against a wall – a man with a whip, the side of a face, another man – and the result re-filmed. In his Super-8 works starting from this period Derek formed an aesthetics based on dissolve, superimposition, softness, sparkle, the dance of the sun

Garden of Luxor (1973), 8-mm film. Postcard of a plant filmed and projected onto a postcard of the Pyramids, then re-filmed.

on the water, texture, slow and exaggerated motion, integration of found and borrowed bits, composition, light acting on matter (as when light shines into the lens directly), the addition of colour (not just natural colour) through filters or video transfer, the creation of metaphors. In short, he developed an array of techniques that tended to induce reverie, mental drift and dream.

Quite different to the feelings of belatedness that had affected his painting, he now felt like a pioneer. His recollections about an early film, *The Art of Mirrors* (1973), show his excitement about this new medium:

> It's some of the most unusual footage I've ever seen . . . The mirrors flashing sunlight into the camera with the light meter set at automatic sends the whole film lurching into negative . . . this is something that could only be done on a Super 8 camera, with its built-in meters and effects. At last we have something completely new.[25]

It was the technical and material effects and possibilities that were so exciting to Derek. This wasn't a visually conventional or straightforward device that simply left the generation of excitement up to the subject-matter: it was the way things could be done and could be made to look that interested Derek. Super-8 brought qualities of colour and possibilities of texture. Both his father and his maternal grandfather, Puttock, had made their own home movies, and so Derek could now prolong the family habit as well as surpass them both, by not only using the medium to document his life (though he did that too, as the posthumous *Glitterbug* of 1994 shows) but also, more importantly, to make art. He was also delighted by the low cost of Super-8, 'the whole thing seemed magical – an instrument to bring dreams to life . . . which cost next to nothing', and he immediately confirms the electrifying nature of this conjunction in a metaphor that reinforced that the medium of film was the modern alchemy: 'The resources were small enough; so if independence were a form of purity, I had my hands on the philosopher's stone.'[26]

In the early years, particularly, he worked on scripts for these films, but as his understanding of the medium's possibilities developed, he eventually realized that he didn't need to work with a script, or even to a narrative. Super-8 cassettes gave three minutes of film each at normal speed, so the film-maker can just film images, symbolism, beautiful sights spontaneously glimpsed, and keep them so that they may be later integrated into a larger project (or not used). Sections of film could thus resemble paintings made earlier and arranged together for an exhibition, or notes used later in a coherent literary project, or poems, even, composed occasionally and collected later into a book where the sequence would provide a structure of meaning constituted from the individual poems but transcending any one of them. Such flexibility, allied to such relative cheapness, amounted to an extraordinary escape from constraints.

Emboldened, perhaps, by his own new artistic purposes, he turned down Ken Russell's offer to design the big-budget film *Tommy* in January 1974. He expressed his thoughts about this in a way that indicated his sense of being part of a community, but that he expected his friends to pull their weight more than they had been doing: 'We're all dead broke, but I refuse to be the soup kitchen any longer.'[27] This was clearly a crucially important decision. In the long run it did not mark the end of his designing for others. In later years his greatest achievement in this line was once again for Russell, when he designed the director's production of the Stravinsky opera based on William Hogarth's print series *The Rake's Progress* in Florence (1982) at impossibly short notice. The action was transposed from William Hogarth's eighteenth-century vision of the city to a twentieth-century London. Derek's designs are characterized by an imposing bold assuredness. The brothel scene frames the action with painted giant male nudes, their closed eyes connoting sleep or death. Further squatting male figures in the background hold their skull-like heads in their hands on either side of a diamond-pane window. All this gives the impression of a Blakean setting, which frames a black space at stage level against which the dwarfed performers sing. The Rake's bed-chamber is perceived between the bony legs and beneath the ribcage of a giant skeletal creature, which conflates the spectacle of extinction with that of death (the stuffed figures of an elk, a gorilla and a giraffe stand around on stage). The whole production was an outstanding critical success, and was extremely well received by the Italian audience. Scenes such as the one in which the Devil appears as 'a drug-dealer in a heavy black leather coat' in Angel underground station, with Hogarth portraits standing in as advertising posters, before exiting by leaping onto the shorting rails in a puff of magnesium smoke, was a tour-de-force of design and staging.[28] The arched tiled interior of the Angel station is reminiscent of the arched tiled interior of the convent in *The Devils*. The success of this production in the discerning homeland of opera was particularly sweet to Derek given his earlier disastrous attempt to design *Don Giovanni*.

Nevertheless the decision he took in January 1974 was ultimately important in the redirection of Derek's cinematic life towards his own films. He hoped that it would galvanize his friend Patrik Steede into action in writing a script. Steede was a friend with whom Derek had been planning a film about St Sebastian for quite some time (it seems that the original idea was Steede's). Derek evidently felt that Steede was rather torpid and feckless about the project during 1973–4, but had no other option than to wait for Steede's script.[29] Derek spent several months of 1974 in New York. He took Super-8 film that was to be included in his first lengthy effort, *In the Shadow of the Sun*. He enjoyed the casual sex, but (as on his visit in 1964) tangled with inexplicable American hypocrisy and found the trip unsatisfying: 'I'm temperamentally unsuited to New York life – my journeys here seem founded in a self-destructive impulse.'[30]

Before we move on from these years, with the beautiful sunlit room at Bankside as their centrepiece, we should consider one more creative effort that appeared in a completely different medium. In 1972 Derek published with the Bettiscombe Press a volume of poetry, *A Finger in the Fishes Mouth*. The reflective silver covers are emblazoned with Derek's signature and the title of the volume written in his own hand. A cover photograph (by Wilhelm von Gloeden) shows a grinning youth in a wide-brimmed straw hat looking at us while holding a flying-fish and touching its mouth with his right index finger. The relationship between the cover and the poems contained in the volume is entirely problematic. A turn of the century Mediterranean world is clearly evoked in some of the content, but if the reflectivity of the cover in tandem with Derek's signature says something about subjectivity and objectivity, then it reflects the inconclusiveness and openness of these crucial elements in the poetry as a whole. In fact the poetry never successfully negotiates this subjective/objective question, with the result that some of the emblematic character of the poems is obfuscated. The influences on Derek's poetry at this stage were Imagism, Surrealism, T. S. Eliot and the Beats. One Beat idea was defined in the goal famously set out by Allen Ginsberg: 'Mind is shapely, art is shapely'. If the psychological (intellectual and emotional) and spiritual preparation of the writer is good enough, then the art will be good. Something of this is also expressed in Jack Kerouac's 'List of Essentials' from his *Belief and Technique of Modern Prose* (1955). It seems as if Derek had not yet achieved full maturation in this difficult goal.

Derek seemed to feel the volume's weakness later: Keith Collins says that he tended to disown this volume, rejecting it as bad poetry.[31] The most extensive discussion so far is that of Steven

Dillon, who analyses the deliberate anomalies in the sequence of the poems ('Poem III' is the fourteenth poem in the sequence, for example) and their word and image character.[32] Each poem consists not only of words, but also of the reproduction of an old postcard, and the pagination is arranged to ensure that each poem has a double-page spread, with the image on the left-hand side and the words on the right. So the book belongs to the period's occasional formal experimentation with what literature is (which led to publication of novels illustrated by photographs, or in the case of B. S. Johnson a novel in which the chapters could be read in any order, so that it was published as unbound sheets in a box rather than bound into a cover).[33]

Derek's use of the images poses extraordinary interpretive problems. For example, he printed his 'Poem I' in the section of *Dancing Ledge* that deals with his sexual awakening with Ron Wright in 1964, and this use seems to make perfect sense since the gardening metaphor blends with that of love as an opiate:[34]

> in the common silence
>   of the world
> the white poppies of
>   my love are dancing

The poem also appears as a song in Derek's draft script for 'Dr John Dee and the Art of Mirrors'.[35] However, what are we to make of the fact that in *A Finger in the Fishes Mouth* he printed the poem near the end of the volume, opposite a photograph of the elderly Henri Matisse, who looks across the space of the pages towards the poem (particularly as we have to identify Matisse ourselves)?

The previous poem, numbered 29, uses a postcard depicting 'A Garden in Luxor' (the same postcard that Derek used in his film of that name). An Egyptian theme is common to several poems in the book. Poem 29 is entitled 'Word Poem Fragments March 64':

Sea minstrel
mistral
howling through the gardenias in the avenue

outside the pine trees and
furze sifting the dust

you are the porter
into forgotten landscapes
        the bend in the road
        the bend in the rock

sighing he put the flower
together
        crushed by the horses hooves
        carefully together
        stamen and sepal
        petal and green stalk
he had instructed the horsemen to pass

        the wall was crumbling
roses blown sown blown
by the wind
        the wind howling through the dwindling mountains

here the courtyard is tiled and the
        tiles are blue from majolica
        and what would Cezanne
        have said of the blues
        and the lapping stacked stones
        thrown and hollowed by the wind

Garden imagery; the erosion of art and nature; the piecing together of fragments in a space of classical antiquity; a reference to modernist art in the context of Egypt (is a break or an underlying continuity implied? Surely the latter: Cézanne would have had something, rather than nothing, to say). All this announces a bundle of Derek's themes, some continuing throughout his life, others being especially prevalent in the early 1970s, when he discovered Super-8 and alchemy at nearly the same time, and often referred to ancient Egypt in his work. For occultists ancient Egypt enjoyed a presumed golden age when esoteric knowledge, art and religion were all grasped together in a unity. Through the blue tiles, the roses, the retrieval of forgotten landscapes, the invocation of the postcard itself as a shifter from the present to those landscapes of one's dreams, Derek begins to piece together an ideal world, susceptible, of course, to the erosions that affect even the mountains, but where possibilities of pleasure are implicit.

The final poem of the book ('Poem VII Farewell') returns to an Egyptian theme via a picture of the Pyramids. The feeling is one of elegy, as the poet sorts through what has been achieved in his volume: 'we have awaited new forms in Italy/ and invented rose gardens/ in the billboard promised land/ the highways have come to nothing'. The elegiac feeling deepens in the final lines:

we are building a marble monument
to cover a grave
the days are numbered
we have proven our loss

4

The Feature Films of the 1970s

In January 1975 Derek met James Whaley, a young graduate with aspirations to become a film producer. Whaley at once expressed interest in the project about St Sebastian. As soon as it looked as if the film was going to move ahead, Derek dumped Patrik Steede from the project. Since the project depended on Steede's script, at the time of the film's release Steede contemplated suing, but contented himself with sending Derek an insult or two instead. Steede had always been a problematic friend. His imagination tended towards the macabre and nihilistic, and Derek might have decided that the project would have had a greater chance of success, given Whaley's sanguine energy, if Steede were not involved. In 1968 Steede's involvement in a group art exhibition instigated by Derek's friend Peter Logan had led to Derek being excluded from the exhibition. He was very upset about this for a while, so dumping Steede from *Sebastiane* might have involved an element of revenge.

So Derek, without ever having had any conventional training in film and without ever having worked as an assistant director, found himself directing a feature film. The early 1970s was a time of experiment, however, and Derek already had some experience making his Super-8 films such as *Death Dance* (1973) and *The Art of Mirrors* (1973). Since the producer and the director were complete novices on larger-scale productions, they intelligently decided to employ an experienced and skilled editor and assistant, Paul Humfress, and it is presumably thanks to him and the small and competent crew that the film looks as good as it does. An Italian friend of Derek's provided access to a part of the coast of Sardinia for filming, and in the summer of 1975 Derek was able to re-create there a dream of antiquity that had been broken in the domain of painting by the discontinuities in practice exemplified by the closing of the antiques room at the Slade ten years before. In the new medium, an isolated outpost of the late Roman Empire took form. For moments at least, this imagining of the antique world became idyllic as men embraced, or created and explored a strange poetry of objects and words.

In and around a remote watchtower on an unspecified Mediterranean shore, Roman soldiers tease and torment each other, partly out of boredom and partly for psycho-sexual reasons. They enjoy making black beetles fight, and they like playing ball in the sea, but they plough into more dangerous problems of power, unrequited love and the creation of victims. Eventually the commanding officer orders one of them, Sebastian, executed. By doing this he seems to be siphoning off a cycle of violence that threatens to engulf the little community.[1] Dom Sylvester Houédard, a friend of Derek's of some years' standing, was consulted over the translation of the script into Latin, but eventually the young American scholar Jack Welch undertook the task. The film is acted entirely in Latin. It features a great deal of male nudity and some homoerotic embraces. Despite, or perhaps because of these elements, the film ran for a year in London (four months at the Gate cinema in Notting Hill, beginning in October 1976, followed by a transfer to the West End) and received widespread release in Britain, where Derek attended openings in York, Manchester, Reading, Bristol and Hull. It is difficult to imagine such a release these days, and not because we have progressed into a better world.

Throughout the film there is an atmosphere of perverted power and bullying within an enclosed all-male society that is familiar to any viewer who went to public school. At the watchtower the

Justin diving for the shell in *Sebastiane* (1976).

commanding officer, Severus, is motivated to condemn Sebastian out of sexual frustration laced with sadism. His decision provokes in a soldier named Max a mad psychotic rejoicing in the death sentence. However, the film is by no means all gloom. There is also an exuberance and humour in it, much of which also centres around the figure of Max (who at one point, for example, eats a black beetle). A strange anomalous figure wearing a leopard-skin and leopard head lurks in the dunes to comic effect. Soldiers frolic in the sea and mess about, pretending to have enormous erections when they wake up in the morning. For Derek and for many viewers the film was a triumph for putting homosexual love on mainstream screens, through the watery embraces of Antony and Adrian. Derek claimed that there was no cinematic precedent for this open and lyrical treatment. The Mediterranean landscape is a huge attraction of this film too. Sebastian's friend Justin dives for a particularly beautiful shell and the two of them listen to it, trying to decipher its messages about gods old and new from far-off places. Sunlight sparkles on seawater. In a ruined cottage Sebastian performs a dance 'of the sun on the water'. And to complete the idyll a flock of goats with bells around their necks passes. Sebastian recites two poems, both evocative of his love for a new young male solar deity. Derek's poems in *A Finger in the Fishes Mouth* used old postcards to complement the words. In *Sebastiane* he is able to accompany the poems with moving pictures. For the first poem, Sebastian washes himself in a courtyard, observed by Severus – so that there is a confusion of eroticisms between the displayed voyeurism and the words of the poem ('he sparkles like the gold in the sacred lapis'). For the second poem, Sebastian gazes into a rockpool in a narcissistic manner.

In coming to terms with *Sebastiane* it helps if we understand that Sebastian is not the hero of this film nor of Derek's imagination. Most critical views assume that he is.[2] Confusion about this has impeded our thinking on the clarity of the film. Sebastian may be the protagonist and the antithesis of Max, but the most sympathetic character is his friend Justin, who tries to protect him and undergoes great suffering for his sake. Derek would not have sympathized with Sebastian, who helped to usher in Christianity, the cult that attempted to suppress homosexuality. Indeed, later in *At Your Own Risk* he makes his attitude very clear: 'Sebastian, the doolally Christian who refused a good fuck, gets the arrows he deserved. Can one feel sorry for this Latin closet case?'[3] Sebastian sublimates his patently homoerotic feelings into godly feelings (his expressed love of God is overtly homoerotic) while refusing actual sexual contact with anyone. He is punished not simply because he's a Christian, but for withholding sex. He seems scared of the joy and loss of control that sexuality entails.

Dramatized in Max and Sebastian are differing pagan and Christian attitudes to the body. The pagan attitude is that the body provides pleasures of various kinds, and might as well be used for what it can yield in this respect. Christianity, anticipating rewards in the afterlife, disparages life in this world. Sebastian's listlessness, his abjection and subjugation, push him to the brink of despising this world because his reward is supposed to come after death. (When Justin tries to shade Sebastian's eyes from the sun during one of the latter's punishments, Sebastian tells him to get out of the way and complains that he doesn't understand.) In worldly human terms Sebastian's attitude is as arid as the landscape around. All this helps to explain the actor Leo Treviglio's apparently lacklustre performance. His recital of the poems, in particular, is anything but arresting or dynamic.

Sebastian doesn't necessarily feel himself abject as a victim. Rowland Wymer has provided a convincing interpretation of the film's final shot. In this shot Derek's wish for a 'poetic, mysterious' film comes through clearly.[4] Wymer interprets it as expressing a union of Sebastian with his solar deity: the shot is made from above Sebastian's point of view as he stands tied to a stake and shot full of arrows, and during it the soldiers all seem to kneel down one by one: however, they do not kneel to Sebastian but, so far as can be discerned, all but one face the declining sun.[5] This shot is exceptional within the film for being filmed through a wide-angle lens rather than a conventional perspectival projection. It even seems to show, in the distant coast and what looks like an island, a rounded earth, perhaps intimating a cosmic vision. In addition, unlike any other shot in the film, its focus is soft.

Once we take in the fact that Sebastian is not the hero, the film is able to yield up a satisfying series of layers of meaning, of interpretation and of feeling. This is not a simple and straightforward narrative. People who are difficult to like become suddenly charming and vice versa. Despite its leisurely pace, the film has no idle moments. After filming ceased in Sardinia, back in London Derek and Paul Humfress discovered that they didn't have enough film for a conventional feature film, and would have to film some more. They staged a cruel orgy in Diocletian's palace, featuring an obscene dance performed by Lindsay Kemp's dance troupe, followed by the killing of a young Christian youth by the biting of his neck. This became the initial scene of the film and is the most Ken Russell-like in its excess. Thereafter the film is aesthetically quite disciplined, via the bareness and dryness of the setting, the absence of built sets, a scanty wardrobe department and minimal use of props.

Derek didn't enjoy making *Sebastiane*. There were difficulties, rows, walk-outs and a struggle with Paul Humfress when he wanted a co-directing credit (which Derek opposed, but which was eventually granted). Derek no doubt felt that as a total novice with considerable responsibility resting on him he was often groping his way, and the experience of learning so much so rapidly must have been exhausting. The experience no doubt left Derek with a desire for the process of film-making to be fun, not simply that the product should be a success. In an interview with Chris Lippard at the end of his life, he said:

> There is not much point in making a film if it is such grim hard work that you say at the end of it: 'I made a good film but we had a hellish time.' I do really believe that one should be able to say 'we had a great time and we actually managed to make a successful film'.[6]

This intimates commercial film-making as really a way of life, rather than just a way of earning a living. After *Sebastiane* Derek began the process of creating an ever-changing group of friends or reliably friendly acquaintances who could help to make the films because they enjoyed working together and with him. The motivation became to ensure that the sets and locations were fun places to work in and that the films depended heavily upon the creative contributions of friends (while ensuring Derek top billing).

The winter of 1975–6 was spent in close collaboration with Humfress editing the film – stretching the available material out to the right length for a feature film. According to Derek, Humfress wanted a 'slow art film' while Whaley wanted a parade of handsome naked young men.[7] Whaley got what he wanted, and Humfress too, mainly because there was no alternative (the material being too scanty for a frenetic pace).

By this time Derek was becoming acknowledged in the world outside *Sebastiane*'s set as a film-maker. In 1976 some of his Super-8 films were screened at the Institute of Contemporary Arts (ICA) and included in a travelling exhibition of the work of a number of experimental British film-makers.

In 1977 the sequence of events that led to the making of his film *Jubilee*, according to Derek, were as follows. Punk had arrived on the streets and in the clubs. He had seen Jordan (born Pamela Rooke), who seemed to epitomize the whole movement, and had become interested in her. She dressed outrageously, she twisted her hair up into a flame-shape, she painted her face for her daily journey on the train into London from Brighton, and she worked at the boutique known as 'Sex' in the King's Road. As part of Punk, shop assistants went out of their way to insult customers, and customers did what they could to trample the clothes, make them dirty or steal them. Derek's interest led him to make a short Super-8 film of Jordan dancing ballet, known as 'Jordan's Dance', which sees her dancing in a tutu at a scene of sacrifice. Books are burning on a bonfire, together with other objects, including a placard of the Union Jack. Present at this burning and dancing stand two other figures wearing masks. One is a mask of Michelangelo's *David*, worn by a naked man. The other figure wears a Death's Head mask. The young man who feeds the fire with books cuts off locks of his own hair to add to the sacrifice. If we construe the two masked figures as connoting Art and Death, perhaps the sacrifice is being performed for them, and celebrated by Jordan's dance. The fire would represent a purification, the consumption of useless clutter. In the background a little apart stands a figure with a paper bag over her head, giving a rather dog-headed profile. A similar figure was used in Derek's Super-8 *The Art of Mirrors*. She probably represents esoteric knowledge.

Sebastiane's producers, Whaley and Malin, decided that Punk could be financially exploited in a feature film, directed by Derek. Given that 'Jordan's Dance' is incorporated almost entire in *Jubilee*, and that the feature film is in some sense built upon it, some questions arise. What is the artistic relationship between the two films? And what sort of film is *Jubilee*? After all, from Whaley and Malin having the idea of making money out of Punk, to the release of the finished film, Derek had to conceive, write and shape something. In fact *Jubilee* is not a film about Punk, nor is it a Punk film. In other words, it neither takes the Punk phenomenon as its subject-matter, nor does it form its structure according to Punk tendencies. (It doesn't for example, try to form itself in emulation of the amateurish-looking yet interesting Punk 'fanzines' of the period. In fact a Super-8 handheld film such as the few minutes Derek took of the Sex Pistols in performance at Andrew Logan's studio might have better lent itself to that purpose. Yet it does take elements of the visual design of the sets from the fanzines.) Given what Whaley and Malin wanted, we should trust Christopher Hobbs's judgement when he states that *Jubilee* was filmed in the idiom of Punk simply because Punk was around at the time.[8] Therefore to leave Punk on one side is to clear the ground better for the question, what sort of film is *Jubilee*?

The film is a good deal more chaste than some of Derek's ideas for it. Manuscript notes proposed 'Alternative Footage':

Donald and Jordan, Film daylight.
Donald fucks Jordan. This in
* fairly naturalistic location corr.
early morning Albert memorial. ArtSex.

Robert or similar massages
Young boy with oil on bed

Jean Mar given a blow job
While he eats a banana.
Hampstead Heath, V. early
Naked > next week

Luciana naked on bed with
Pussy cat between legs

Punk boy masturbating in front of
Mirror in leather gear

Change Luciana and cat
                               to panther
if possible ———————>

Old woman masturbating
<the reactionary clique is dead>
 The Last of England [9]

And at this point in the notes we realize that these ideas are merely
for the opening credit sequence.

   The film takes its eventual title (it had different working titles)
from the Queen's Jubilee in 1977. In this year the Queen, the royal
family and elements of national and local government attempted
to persuade the population to celebrate the Queen's Jubilee with
street parties and communal meals of the kind that had celebrated
the end of the Second World War, and that had been last seen
perhaps at the Queen's coronation early in the 1950s. There were
also naval parades and other official and organized events. In the
meantime the economy was taking a downturn and the nation had

recently had to behave like a Third World country by taking a loan from the International Monetary Fund. All this had provoked widespread gloom. *Jubilee*, then, is on one level Derek's response to Queen Elizabeth II having been on the throne for a quarter of a century. Yet this hardly characterizes what sort of film it is. In fact it has never been properly stated that the film is a dystopia and a satire. As a *dystopia*, a pessimistic form of 'no-place' (*utopia*), it shows a city filled with random violence, no law and order, government abdicated or ineffectual, the world made into prey for the powerful, a totalitarian countryside holding old dictators in comfort. In depicting this the film imagines a future that had not yet in 1977 come into being. The chief target of Derek's satire is capitalism, with its thirst to own and profit from everything, and centred here in the impresario-figure Borgia Ginz, played with great brio by Jack Birkett. He progressively buys up Bod's female gang ('our little gang of media heroines' as Derek described them later[10]), lives in Buckingham Palace and owns the media. At the end of the film the 'heroines' take him for a country holiday, where in retirement at Longleat House they find Adolf Hitler muttering in German that he was the 'greatest painter of the twentieth century'.

Targets of attack in *Jubilee* thus include the quality of the State (gauged by the behaviour of its policemen but also here by its monarchy) as well as capitalism, which seeks to exploit and destroy art. A satire exposes to ridicule and irony the vice, folly, abuses and evils that it chooses to target. Satire thus needs humour, and despite its dystopic character there is an unruly humour in *Jubilee* that surfaces in unexpected places (the actress Claire Davenport put into a Red Army uniform as the totalitarian guard at the border of Dorset is funny, for example, as spectacle and as concept). Derek likened the film to the Ealing comedies of the 1950s: 'in our film the laughter is nervous, but it is there'.[11] Yet a satire also needs to be pointed by being able to refer to merit. A sense needs to come across of an alternative to the corrupted world that is being condemned, and the alternative has to be recognized as good (in some moral or philosophical sense) for the satire to take its stand upon it. In *Jubilee* the most obvious example of this comes over in the framing device, in which a glamorous Queen Elizabeth I is entertained by a real magician, John Dee, who is able to call up a real spirit, Ariel. Here the Elizabethan sixteenth century acts as a golden age which shows by contrast the pitiful state of the projected near-future. Derek might have wished that he could possess and inhabit this depicted world of actual magic, but knew that he could only do so in the imagination: the world of Elizabeth and Dee here is an intangible fantasy. So this nostalgic displacement is supplemented by a good alternative within the dystopic future of Queen Elizabeth II's reign. The characters Sphinx (Karl Johnson) and Angel (Ian Charleson) are not murderous nihilists but roving intelligences, commenting sceptically on life and society around them, trying to persuade The Kid (Adam Ant's character) not to mess about with Crabs nor to sign up with Borgia Ginz, befriending the lonely artist Viv, and pursuing their own queer relationship. They, with Viv, represent the rational element striving to keep its feet in the dystopic murk.

In published commentaries on *Jubilee* it is noticeable that the importance of Angel, Viv and Sphinx in this respect is most often misunderstood.[12] Critics suggest that a key theme in the film is the absence of love. It is true that Crabs's search for love is satirical. She murders her sexual pick-up Happy Days, and then there is a scene in which she, Bod and Mad throw the body into the Thames mud. Crabs expresses regret at not finding love but Bod assures her that 'love snuffed it with the hippies'. Before this scene is even over, however, we hear Angel singing 'my love is like a red red rose' and then cut to a scene of him lying in bed with Sphinx who holds Viv in his arms. When the song ends, Angel tells Sphinx that he loves him. Sphinx replies that he loves Angel too, and Viv tells both the boys that she loves them. It seems that love does survive after all, and it resides in homosexual society (perhaps bisexual) and in art.

The three characters thus represent the survival of the good in a corrupted world, and this gives considerably more strength to two significant elements. One of these is what Viv says about artists. She says that artists steal the world's energy, that the people who own the world drive artists into corners (because energy is dangerous) and that the only hope is 'to recreate ourselves as artists and release the energy for all'. Here 'energy' seems to mean soul, or life force, and Viv states what is Derek's own view. He returns to it repeatedly in his films and writings, and this moment in *Jubilee* is the important theme's first appearance in his work. As we saw from *Dancing Ledge* in the last chapter, Derek repeatedly equates art with theft (theft of everyday creativity from the world: a lesson derived *a contrario* from the example of Robin Noscoe, spreading creativity around with his Art Hut, his respect for the craft tradition, his house and his attitude to the necessity of practical skills). Here Viv gives a revolutionary view: the artists' revolution will not be made by serving the political revolution under that latter's own

Where love lives: Sphinx, Viv and Angel in *Jubilee* (1978).

terms. It must instead be a revolution about art and artists which might then be able to effect (or contribute to) a broader liberation.

The second significant element resides in the associations of Angel's and Sphinx's names. 'Sphinx' directly implies esoteric knowledge, the Jarmanian dream of ancient Egypt as a place with no gaps between devotion, knowledge and action.[13] The name of 'Angel' connects the action of the dystopia to the framing device of Queen Elizabeth I's world. Here John Dee repeatedly calls Ariel an 'angel'. Thus there is an implied link between the two characters which allows Ariel's utterances about the world an additional resonance. 'Equality exists not for the gods' sake, but for man's', he says. And 'Consider the world's diversity and worship it.' These utterances are obviously not intended by the film-maker to seem out of the reach of practical life in 1978.

A central though quiet place in the film is thus found for a dramatization of Derek's own attitude to creative activity and artistic energy. In relation to this, some other elements of the punk phenomenon fall into place, such as punk music's claim to offer an alternative to a music industry that had hopelessly sold out and completely lost its artistic edge. This was the era of the Bay City Rollers, if anyone remembers them, of Alvin Stardust, of the Bee Gees singing high-pitched and vacuous disco music, of Rod Stewart, formerly of The Faces, 'Sailing' to a cosy berth in Hollywood's 'easy listening' sector. Derek in *Jubilee* expresses scepticism as to whether anyone can resist being bought off, given how financing is structured. So long as profiteering remains the highest good, rather than aesthetic quality of the product or value of the process, the situation remains prejudiced against creative activity.

One footnote on *Jubilee* casts light on these questions. Vivienne Westwood, the fashion designer, went to see the film and wrote an essay on it in the form of a letter to Derek that was printed on a T-shirt. She appreciated the release of creative energy that his way of making the film had caused and relied on:

Good – the low budget, independent, using friends, non-equity aspect. Good that the non-equity members weren't required to act but allowed to say their lines as if reading from a little book inside their heads, because what happened by result of this acting, as against some acting ability was that the performances depended for strength on how much humanity the people behind the role possessed.[14]

This passage shows that Westwood understood and appreciated Derek's practical application of his idea that artists need to re-invent themselves as artists to release creative energy in the world. However, she didn't understand anything about the Elizabethan framing device. In particular she rejected – perhaps for ideological reasons, who knows? – Ariel's call for diversity and equality. She also filled the T-shirt with caustic and gratuitous insults about Derek and his sexuality and at one point solemnly tried to teach him his job.

However, Derek had his revenge. After writing on the T-shirt that 'nationalism is vile and Elizabeth II is a commercial con trick', Westwood was offered an OBE in 1992 by Elizabeth II. Derek wrote in his journal, later published as *Smiling in Slow Motion*,

> Vivienne Westwood accepts an OBE, dipsy bitch. The silly season's with us: our punk friends accept their little medals of betrayal, sit in their vacuous salons and destroy the creative – like the woodworm in my dresser . . . I would love to place a man-sized insectocutor, lit with royal-blue, to burn up this clothes moth and her like.[15]

Or, as Borgia Ginz prophesies in the film, 'They all sign up, in the end.'

Jubilee employs a strategy of internal pairing of characters and events, all of which tend to point or reinforce the satire. John Dee's garden in which the film opens, a haven of peace and quiet, contrasts with the film's second garden, made entirely of plastic by the sardonic ex-soldier Max. As this second garden is barren it serves to underline by contrast with Dee's denatured character of the modern world. Amyl Nitrate (played by Jordan) performs two dances. Her ballet dance on Super-8 vividly dramatizes her memory or fantasy of her wish to be a ballerina. Her second dance as she sells out to Borgia Ginz is a grotesque version of 'Rule, Britannia!' This powerful contrast shows artistic aspirations being suborned and bought up by capital to be transformed into the grotesque. On another level, of course, Amyl's second dance is also art. It satirizes the post-imperial posturings of Elizabeth II's Jubilee year. But within the narrative of the film Borgia Ginz harnesses a tawdry jingoism for his profit-making purposes. Another kind of doubling in *Jubilee* features in-jokes that relate to the film-maker's earlier oeuvre. The sardonic ex-soldier Max who complains that there's not enough killing in the army is played by Neil Kennedy, the actor who played Max the mad soldier in *Sebastiane*. In *Jubilee* he eats a caterpillar rather than a beetle. And the curvaceous Luciana Martinez is tied to a lamp-post in a posture echoing that of Sebastian in the earlier film; there is even a tower nearby: the tower of Pisa, seen in effigy in an advertisement hoarding.

The film's most serious point concerns the spiritual versus the material, and emerges partly from the strategy of internal pairing. In Elizabeth I's time alchemy and occult knowledge are alive, and can be seized: Elizabeth II's Britain is materialist in a philosophical as well as an economic sense. Even the nation's religions can be bought. As Borgia Ginz exclaims in another of his memorable sayings, 'Without Progress life would be unbearable. Progress has taken the place of Heaven!' He means, of course, the idea of progress, a new form of opium to be manipulated by capital. The rush to materialism in thought as well as life, together with the wholesale dismissing of the past, enraged Derek the bohemian.

He told Colin McCabe that he was 'furious' while he was writing *Jubilee*: the punk rebellion had unleashed something in him that went right back to his schooldays.[16] Some of this underlying anger wells to the surface in the film's ultra-violence: the killing of the policemen, Bod's orgasm-fuelled strangulation of Lounge Lizard, the policemen's killing of The Kid. The resulting film contains in its gutsy energy a range of Derek's long-standing concerns, motifs and preoccupations, from an element of ultra-violence, to a love of the Dorset coast, to an insistence on the centrality of homosexual love, to a liking for putting film to music that directly prefigures his work in pop promos. To the reviewer for *Vogue* the film was 'very contemporary and oddly attractive . . . shows an acutely sympathetic understanding, not of how people behave, but of how they dream'. The influential u.s. magazine *Variety* praised its 'brutal and lyrical vision . . . electric performances, operatic elegance and narrative sophistication . . . Jarman unravels the nation's social history in a way other features haven't even attempted.'[17] There were other laudatory reviews in the *Evening Standard*, *Time Out* and the *Evening News*.

By the time *Jubilee* opened in February 1978 Derek was working on the idea of a film about the Italian painter Michelangelo Merisi, better known as Caravaggio (1573–1610). After watching *Sebastiane*, the art dealer Nicholas Ward-Jackson conceived that Derek would be a good person to make a film of Caravaggio's life, and was introduced to Derek by a mutual friend, the painter Robert Medley. German art historians in the 1970s were hypothesizing that Caravaggio had been queer or bisexual, so Derek was seen as someone who could do justice to him and reclaim a queer life from historical obscurity.[18] Caravaggio's effect on painting had been enormous: he was singlehandedly the inventor of the shadowy *tenebroso* Baroque painting that spread rapidly in the early seventeenth century to become an international style, adopted by such famous names as Velázquez and Rembrandt. Yet Caravaggio's name was less famous than theirs or those of Michelangelo, Raphael, Titian, Dürer or Leonardo. A contract was signed and Derek began work. He spent much of the summer of 1978 in Italy, studying Caravaggio's paintings and writing the first version of a script for the film. However, two events happened in rapid succession that led to *Caravaggio* being put aside.

In August 1978 Derek's beloved mother died after an illness of eighteen years. Derek was 36. His account of her death in *Dancing Ledge* is dressed up by implying that he and his sister Gaye were present at the moment of death, where in reality neither of them were, and by sheer accident her husband Lance was absent too.[19] In *Dancing Ledge* 'Derek' asks her, 'Are you alright?' and she answers, 'Of course not, silly, but you are.'[20] This anecdote seems unlikely on a factual level, but Derek no doubt felt it represented a truth about his mother. It shows her deflecting an expressed concern about herself back to the other person. She refuses to talk about her needs and attempts to support her children even in her own distress. He seemed to be able to look past her brave face to an assumed generosity of spirit, an attempt to create good cheer and optimism in others through her own energy and efforts.

This huge emotional blow called forth in Derek a stupendous honesty about his feelings: 'When Ma died I felt elation.'[21] He immediately follows this sentence with a set of conventional thoughts about his mother having been happy in her humble life, and so forth, but he cannot completely camouflage the exultant energy within 'elation'. Perhaps his queer life felt freer with the disappearance of parental authority, the evaporation of potential conflicts that authority might cause and with them the memory of past conflicts. This might explain an otherwise puzzling juxta-position in *Dancing Ledge*, where he includes an account of being gazed at by a handsome young man in a restaurant, and gazing back, immediately after the paragraphs describing his mother's death. There is no principle of connection between the two episodes and the difference in tone is striking. The gazing incident seems entirely concerned with self, the described feelings being extremely narcissistic, but perhaps the incident also exemplifies a defiance of death and a return to life's possibilities.

Shortly after his mother's death there landed on Derek's desk a positive response to his proposal to make a film of William Shakespeare's play *The Tempest*. The production arrangements were in the hands of Don Boyd's new company, which already specialized in producing challenging films such as Alan Clarke's *Scum* and Ron Peck's *Nighthawks*, and were different from those provided by Whaley and Malin. There was more money, and a professionalism, particularly from Sarah Radclyffe, who went on to become one of the more important producers in British film. Derek knew the play well. He had studied it on his English course at King's as an undergraduate, and since then had formed ideas for staging the play at the Roundhouse (a platform for radical theatre in the 1970s). He had also deconstructed the play at least as far as forming a version in which a mad Prospero is confined in an asylum and plays all the parts himself. Derek's film, released in 1980, was thus his third interpretation, one that carved up Shakespeare's text to an extraordinary extent.

The action of Shakespeare's play shows Prospero, a magician, cast away on a desert island with his daughter, Miranda, and living in a cave. The only other inhabitant of the island is the 'ugly and deformed' Caliban, whom Prospero has enslaved to perform menial tasks such as finding firewood. However, Prospero has also enslaved a faery spirit, Ariel, whom he obliges to perform tasks of magic. Ariel creates a tempest which wrecks, or appears to wreck, a ship carrying Prospero's usurping brother together with the King of Naples, his son and brother. The son (Ferdinand) washes ashore, is treated badly as a test of worth by Prospero, and engages to marry Miranda. The rest of the royal party make their way to shore to be humbled by Ariel's servants. Two sailors wash ashore, and

Caliban exhorts them to murder Prospero and take over the island. This threat is easily defeated by Ariel. There is a masque in honour of the betrothal of Ferdinand and Miranda, after which Prospero forgives the royal party, dismisses Caliban, renounces magic, sets Ariel free and sails for retirement in Milan, whence he came.

Derek cut up the text ruthlessly, suppressing huge amounts of dialogue and transferring parts of what remained to different moments in the play. He intended that the corpse of the play left over should be cinematic, cinema at its best being highly visual and spare with dialogue. In doing this he was intent on converting the play into a film (this is not the same as the idea of filming a play, a concept that I shall come back to in relation to *Edward II*). In the end he cut too much. Three quarters of the way through the film enters a slack area where in order to understand the action viewers really need more information about the triangle formed by Miranda, Ferdinand and Prospero, together with a better idea of Prospero's intentions. The forgiveness of the royal party is also skimmed over. As a result the film is really only intelligible to people who know the play already, and Derek's purpose of turning it into a film fails on the level of plot or story.

Filming took place in the cold snowy winter of 1978–9 at Bamburgh on the Northumberland coast and at Stoneleigh Abbey in Warwickshire. There the large late Baroque Georgian wing, described by Derek's old teacher Pevsner and Alexandra Wedgwood as 'mighty rather than festive', and made even less festive by a fire in 1960, provided an equivalent for Prospero's cave.[22] Continuing his process of trying to find a party of right-minded collaborators, Derek re-employed some of the cast of *Jubilee*: Jack Birkett gives a wonderful vigorous performance as Caliban, Karl Johnson played Ariel, Toyah Willcox was Miranda, Helen Wallington-Lloyd a dwarf servant of Ariel's and Claire Davenport the witch Sycorax. The skilful and confident Peter Middleton was director of photography. The exterior shots on the beach were filmed through a blue filter in broad daylight to give a twilight effect, and the result is a remarkable *grisaille* which makes the scenes strange, emphasizes their compositions and foreshortens spatial relationships. Just as remarkably, the film starts by employing amateur film from the 1930s showing a sailing ship in heavy seas. This continues the process of embedding an allegedly inferior-quality film within the final product that Derek had used with 'Jordan's Dance' in *Jubilee*. There are therefore three qualities of film used: the normal 16-mm interior shots at Stoneleigh, the blue-filtered exterior 16-mm shots and the 8-mm amateur footage of the ship. Each is valued by the film-maker for its individual properties, rather than because they all coalesce into a seamless whole.

Derek replaced Shakespeare's elaborate betrothal masque with a two-part sequence. First there is a sailors' dance that is often erroneously described as 'camp'. (Camp is the costume Trinculo wears to the dance, a costume worthy of Andrew Logan's 'Alternative Miss World' parties.) This was followed by the veteran singer Elisabeth Welch singing a Cole Porter song, 'Stormy Weather'. Michael O'Pray rightly claims this as having a 'majestic quality' and being 'one of the great scenes of British cinema'.[23] Derek always claimed that his film-making was an extension of painting, and we get some inkling of what that means when Welch turns away at the end of the song and her gold and white costume goes out of focus for a prolonged moment in a gorgeous effect of pure colour and abstract form. The way the film continues from here is revealing of another aspect of Derek's sensibility. We cut to a scene of Prospero sleeping and Ariel creeping around in the same room, but now full of dead leaves: this is a weird transformation from the pristine hall of the masque. Ariel runs up the stairs to freedom to disappear halfway up in the sound of swans' wings. Prospero's voice-over says that all the spirits have melted into air and he gives a version of the famous 'cloud-capped towers' speech. His eyes remain closed and his face unmoving as he concludes it

Elisabeth Welch and Derek Jarman on the set of *The Tempest* (1979).

with the words 'we are such stuff/ as dreams are made on and our little life/ is rounded with a sleep'. That is the end of the film. This last part picks up on some earlier undercurrents to deliver a heavily elegiac effect and, perhaps surprisingly for a play that features a wedding, from Derek's version death emerges as a strong theme.[24] Immediately after Prospero's last words there is a cut to the black-and-white caption:

> This film is dedicated to the memory of
> Elizabeth Evelyn Jarman

and the credits reel past in silence. We could therefore be justified in reading the film as a tribute to Derek's mother. He wrote later that since his father had concealed the whereabouts of her ashes, her 'only memorial' was his *Tempest*.[25] The song that Elisabeth Welch sings is about loss, but is the song of a loving spirit, and the atmosphere in which she sings it suggests that love is redemptive. Derek's mother loved Shakespeare, too: Derek carried with him vivid memories from boyhood of his mother delighting her children by leaping onto the kitchen table and reciting martial speeches from *Henry v* that she had learned at school.

One of the great pleasures of Derek's film is its spare lighting. The film reveals a world of shadows and lights – often candlelight in dark spaces. The action takes place in the shadowy baroque world invented in art by Caravaggio. The energy of his naturalism and his light/dark contrasts drive the visual design of the film. Characters are dimly lit from one side, or wander through beams of light in echoing shadows. And as in Caravaggio's paintings there is always more than simply dramatically lit naturalism: deep human feeling and pathos well up from the characters.

So in Derek's *The Tempest* the stupid aspirations of Caliban and his pains emerge all the more powerfully in raking light from his obscure setting, as does the worn-out depression of Ariel and the figure of Prospero trying to drive his purposes onwards, or Miranda, weeping over her father's cruelty to Ferdinand while petting a butterfly. This conceptualization – the use of baroque space in which the characters' emotions live all the more vividly, constitutes the heart of the film and the reason it grips us. The film is Derek's first homage to the great late-Renaissance painter. Someone of Derek's aesthetic sensibilities and his interest in esoteric knowledge might have been struck by the fact that *The Tempest* was written the year following Caravaggio's death, and Derek's film was taking shape in the Baroque architecture of a house in Shakespeare's home county.

What about the theme of the artists' need to reinvent themselves as artists and release creative energy into the world that was so quietly stated in *Jubilee*? Arguably it emerges again in *The Tempest*, applying in two ways. First it is figured in the story. While Prospero has been traditionally interpreted as an artist, in Derek's film Ariel is explicitly signalled as an artist too. In particular, the masque is shown to be his production, a response to a mere general order of Prospero's. When he enters the hall at the beginning of the masque the latter says admiringly, 'my tricksy spirit!' It is even arguable that the song 'Stormy Weather', featuring the lines 'I'm weary all the time' and sung by a spirit conjured up by Ariel, amounts to Ariel's own song; he touches his mouth in a peculiar way during the singing. Soon after this Miranda and Ferdinand kiss, so an alternative suggestion could be that Ariel's power extends to them. Thus the escape of Ariel to freedom could be allegorized as the escape of creative energy from the sole dominion of the artist back into the world. The other way that the theme impinged on the making of *The Tempest* was behind the camera. In all the production and creative work that went into the making of the film, Derek felt that he had achieved what he wanted by trusting the people who were working with him and encouraging them to do what they wanted. His creative *virtù* had been to unleash their creativity, and in this way his film had been made. The set of *The Tempest* was a particularly happy place to work. While everyone worked hard, there was also a party atmosphere at Stoneleigh Abbey, where the cast and crew lodged as well as it being their place of work for four weeks. Derek asserted that their working practice had a basis in mutual respect:

> I take over completely. What happens is the opposite from the normal film set. I know exactly what I want to do. The situation has been created so everyone can do whatever they want to do because it will be exactly what I want to happen. It's like throwing a party: you just go along and choose the right people for your party and you stick by them, then it doesn't go wrong.[26]

Post-production on the film took place in 1979 and the film was screened at the London Film Festival before being released in 1980. After *The Tempest*, for Derek everything changed.

5

Painting, Writing, Pop Promos

The year 1979 saw several events that were to affect Derek's life
profoundly for years afterwards. In the summer he moved out of
Butler's Wharf to a one-room flat in an unprepossessing modernist
block in the Charing Cross Road. A few weeks later Butler's Wharf
burned in one of the mysterious Thames-side fires. The new flat, in
Phoenix House (surely an auspicious name), was small and unsuit-
able for painting. It is hard to avoid the thought that moving out
of the studio to the flat was a sign – to Derek himself as much as
to others – that he was now a film-maker rather than a painter and
so did not need a painter's studio any more.[1] Moreover, the sign
suggested that he was a maker of feature films, given how the early
Super-8s and even much of *Jubilee* had been filmed in his studio.
In a later published interview he said, 'from the age of eight I was
going to be a painter . . . it didn't cross my mind until I'd been
making films for five years, in fact until *The Tempest*, that I was a
film-maker now'.[2] Ironically, perhaps, he now ran into a hiatus in
the making of feature films and it was not until after a full-scale
return to Super-8 that the next feature film, *Caravaggio*, would be
made. Added to this was a further irony in the fact that his major
artistic work of the early 1980s was an exhibition of paintings.

The year 1979 also saw the election of a Conservative government
led by Margaret Thatcher. This government for better or worse
changed Britain profoundly. Initially, at least, it did untold harm to
the country, and a series of cynical and pusillanimous subsequent

governments by the Conservatives and 'New Labour' have failed to correct some of Thatcher's worst mistakes, notably in the domains of taxation and the balance of power between labour and capital controlled by trade union legislation. More generally her ideology fundamentally changed the idea of British civilization: she denied that society existed, denigrated the concept of public services, demanded that everything should be, in the phrase of the period, 'cost effective', downplayed cabinet government and greatly increased centralized control while hypocritically demeaning 'too much government'. Before too long Derek was to find himself in the forefront of one campaign in the struggle against the Thatcher government's overbearing deployment of power. For the rest of his life he lived under Conservative rule.

In 1979 Derek also made his first pop promotional films (which would now be termed 'music videos' although they were shot on film, not video). These were for Marianne Faithfull, who released the album *Broken English* in that year. Derek's film for her title song makes it even angrier than is the song alone. He cuts between film of fascist leaders and parades, war footage, shots of police attacking demonstrators, refugees, the Blitz and film of a Buddhist monk burning himself to death in protest against the Vietnam War (this shot is synchronized with the refrain of the song, 'What are you fighting for?'). All is black and white. The threat of nuclear annihilation in the shape of a hydrogen bomb test is set at the beginning to dominate everything. The weight of all this in the two and a half minutes of the song is all but overwhelming, and images of dance competitions and space invaders games imply the militarization of civil life. The implication of the song, that the militarization of the twentieth century has broken England, is greatly enhanced by Derek's powerful montage. The film for Faithfull's 'The Ballad of Lucy Jordan' is gentler, but not more optimistic. In Super-8, it features Faithfull walking by night in Piccadilly Circus, superimposed on film of a woman's banal and maddening domestic drudgery consonant with the words of the song. The third short film, 'Witch's Song', features love-making between a man and a female impersonator in one of Derek's dockland–wasteland settings. The song, which sets up, and resists, the probing condemnation of sexual infidelity, had been written for Faithfull by the poet Heathcote Williams, Prospero in Derek's *The Tempest*.

From this point on pop promos were outlets for Derek's creative energies and ways of making much-needed money. He made 22 over a period of 15 years. The accepted view is that those for The Smiths and The Pet Shop Boys are the finest, especially The Pet Shop Boys' 'It's a Sin' (1987) and The Smiths' 'The Queen is Dead'. Indeed, 'The Queen is Dead' (made with Richard Heslop) is a masterly little Jarman Super-8 transferred to video, packed with energy from both the music and the new editing techniques made possible by the explosion of music video in the 1980s, and that Derek extols in various places: a phantasmagoria of high-speed cutting, superimposition, partial superimposition of colour on black and white and vice versa, negative and solarization effects.[3] 'The Queen is dead boys', the song tells us: 'the Church only wants your money . . . life is very long when you're lonely.' Music and film together present a revision of what Britain is. Derek's film for The Smiths' 'Panic' shares the same atmosphere, locating it plumb in the centre of London on a bridge over the Thames. The collaborative nature of the work for The Smiths, involving Richard Heslop, John Maybury, Cerith Wyn Evans and Christopher Hughes as co-makers of the films, perpetuates Derek's concern that artists need to spread the opportunities for creativity by re-inventing themselves. The Pet Shop Boys' 'It's a Sin' is a memorable short film in the aesthetic that the musicians themselves chose after viewing Derek's *Caravaggio*. There are plenty of flames, an element that Derek had discovered in the early Super-8s to be very photogenic. Taken with the words of the song, the film suggests the burden of guilt and condemnation of desire by traditional (Christian) societies. The song allows for imaginative participation by both queer viewers and heterosexuals (in some societies heterosexual adultery is still a crime and a sin, for example). This work also led Derek to produce the stage show for The Pet Shop Boys, and film it (1989), although, harassed by ill-health at the time, he found this an ordeal which did not end satisfactorily.

However, these small films (after those for Marianne Faithfull) lay in the future, a counter-attack against the cultural politics of the Thatcher era. In 1980 *The Tempest* was released, and September saw Derek back in New York for the disappointing opening of the film, blighted by a hostile and hysterical review in the *New York Times*. According to a long-standing friend and collaborator, Ken Butler, Derek was always impatient, hasty to get on to the next project, and he now became greatly frustrated at the failure of *Caravaggio* to progress to the production stage.[4] In the meantime he worked on scripts, writing and rewriting ('Neutron' with Lee Drysdale, for example) and interesting various acquaintances in the possibilities of projects that were destined to remain unmade. The theatre maestro Steven Berkoff held out promise of collaboration; Derek flew to Switzerland to talk to David Bowie about involvement.

Developing scripts is of course the conventional way of inaugurating film projects in the studio world. Films are sold on the basis of scripts, which are then customarily changed and rewritten before the film is ever made. This brings up the question of what is, therefore, changing hands? If the script is to be changed so often, where is the property? Later on, and no doubt because of his frustrations in the 1980s, Derek became extremely sceptical about this method. An essentially visual medium is bought and sold on the basis of words. Moreover, the words will be thrown out, replaced, changed, reversed in meaning, added to and generally mangled by a variety of hands. Where, in the toils of this process, is the place for a conception of film as a moving visual/auditory art? Suffice it to say that before *Caravaggio* at last moved to production Derek had evolved a completely different approach to cinema.

The script, Derek said in 1984, becomes the first stage of censorship. Added to this, 'narrative' – so driven by scripts, in that they serve conversion into 'treatments' that convey narrative better than any other element – 'is the first trap of commercial cinema'.[5] This analysis came later, but the seeds of it were sown in the struggle of the early 1980s to advance *Caravaggio*, or, failing that, 'Neutron'. Thoughts about censorship might have been refined by Derek's friendship with Genesis P. Orridge of Throbbing Gristle. Introduced by James Mackay in 1980, the two assisted each other with their projects. Derek filmed Orridge's 'Psychic Rally in Heaven' in return for Throbbing Gristle providing the soundtrack (through improvisation) for Derek's *In the Shadow of the Sun*.

In the Shadow of the Sun was a consummation of Derek's Super-8 work up to that time, incorporating, for example, 'The Art of Mirrors' and other early work. The film's basis is superimposition. To make it Derek projected two of his earlier films simultaneously onto a postcard, and filmed the result with his Nizo 8-mm camera. As a result the images in the final film move and quiver, and in them figures and objects pulse and shimmer. The focus is soft and approximative. During the re-filming he also used a variety of coloured filters to cause overall colour effects, partly to bind sequences together into larger wholes. The film features many close-ups of fires. A flickering background resolves itself sooner or later as a landscape (that of his early film 'Journey to Avebury', 1972). There are large close-ups of men's faces, and we can make out a ritual involving a bound man lying on the ground in a maze of fire. In one sequence the greatly enlarged image of the postcard of the Pyramids that was used in *A Finger in the Fishes Mouth* forms the background. The film contains many meanings, but they are beyond any narrative level. Depending on the relative values of light and dark at any moment in the two projected films, strange things happen: the ritual seems part of the time to be taking place in a derelict urban site, and part of the time in the countryside, with instantaneous 'moves' between the two. The background can suddenly become the foreground while what used to be the foreground fades into the background. The resulting film is hypnotic and beautiful, with a resonant suggestive echoing score. It includes a shot from *The Devils* that Derek filmed off a cinema screen in New York, superimposed on the ashes of a fire. A wizard, or perhaps God, appears (Christopher Hobbs). Sequences dissolve into an abstract effect of light granules or patches that gradually resolve into light reflecting off water, but for a while the abstracted light looks like film of a nebula or solar system (we've seen one a little earlier in the film, the orange background to a silhouette of Atlas holding up the planet).[6] The film becomes elemental, cosmic, raising questions of what human life and the life of the universe are.

The last stage, made possible by a grant from Berlin, was to transfer the film to 16 mm for projection in cinemas. It was screened at the Berlin Film Festival in 1981 and had a strong effect, at least on its own maker: the film's 'blaze of impressionistic colour' burst out in front of 'a large audience' in a cinema impressing him profoundly.[7] He had produced an extraordinarily dynamic form of moving pictures. This experience, and the evidence of an appreciative audience, confirmed what Derek already knew about the possibilities of cinema. It showed that while he pushed scripts around there was another more direct way of working that depended on exploiting the material properties of the image-making process with a painter's enquiring sensibility. During the 1970s Derek's Super-8 work had tended to throw up ideas that were eventually realized in feature films. All three of them had germinated from ideas for Super-8. With *In the Shadow of the Sun* came a clear intimation of a different possibility: that audiences would enjoy seeing Super-8 used for the sake of its inherent aesthetic properties, and for the transformations the pictures went through as they shifted up in gauge to 16 mm. Their qualities of blurred outlines and approximativeness became less blemishes to be shunned in favour of the crystal clarity of conventional film than elements to be prized for their suggestive possibilities.

In several places Derek blames the new television channel, Channel Four, for his inability to fund *Caravaggio* in these years.[8] It is also often stated by various sources that *The Tempest*'s failure in the USA was a big contributing factor.[9] However, none of Derek's films had done well in the USA, and a more important impediment to progress came at home in Britain, when the Treasury squashed the mechanism by which Don Boyd's creative accountant had financed *The Tempest* and other films produced by Boyd's company.[10] The system, which was of course perfectly legal, depended on delaying tax payments by investors until the film showed a profit. In the event of a loss, larger tax write-offs (larger than the initial investments) came into play. The Treasury regarded this as a loophole and introduced legislation to stop it, thus destroying a good way of financing films outside the studio system, which avoided any strong influence on content exercised by individual investors. The system was inherently non-commercial in that it didn't matter whether films made profits. They didn't need to be driven by commercialism and by the lust for 'success' to be measured by financial returns. (Another film industry non sequitur, of course, measures artistic success by money. A money-making film becomes a 'good' film.)

The year 1981 has some claim to be Derek's emptiest. After the epiphany in Berlin in March, April saw *In the Shadow of the Sun* screened at the ICA, and May found Derek in Cannes trying to whip up funding for the *Caravaggio* project. Much time was spent bothering about scripts, discussing, writing and rewriting. Towards the end of the year he was invited to participate in a group art exhibition with his friends at the B2 Gallery in Wapping, which occasioned a return to painting for him. On a deeper level he was more out of touch with the values of British society than ever before, largely because Mrs Thatcher was reconstructing those values to make profit-taking the sole good. Ultimately he was to find that the way back in to a broader engagement with society around him, and therefore to a sense of belonging within it, was through cultural–political opposition and protest.

For men defined as homosexual (a modern word) by the society that surrounds them it goes without saying that to fulfil one's nature would be to defy the prejudices and laws of one's society.[11] A line of descent from Simeon Solomon and Oscar Wilde to Allen Ginsberg could be constructed to exemplify this. One thinks of Keith Vaughan's lonely and calmly despairing suicide, perhaps an example of the risk involved in failure to defy and contest vigorously enough.[12] The liberalization in 1967 of the laws that attempted to control sexual activity meant that Derek was no longer classified as a criminal (although legal inequities and enormous struggles for social acceptance remained). For a few years in the liberal 1970s it seemed that the cultural space of cinema could be occupied successfully and without too much difficulty. The Conservative turn that Britain took in 1979 meant that Derek had to become oppositional to his society not solely over the question of sexual activity and its acceptance but over a very broad front indeed – perhaps several fronts embracing film, art, authorship and indeed eventually life, as he became a famous name reified through the newspapers and television. In the early 1980s, when she was not denying that society exists, Thatcher was redefining it in such a way that only shareholders of private or publicly traded companies benefited from its existence. With the economic squeeze caused by government-induced recession (interest rates were put up to 17 per cent) came a cultural politics of Thatcherite intolerance and intransigence targeted at the public sector; trade unions (especially); the idea of public service; education; and, involving television, film and art, almost any activity which involved any degree of public funding, no matter how indirect. Derek's struggle during these years to continue along his path as a painter and maker of feature films was also an example of a struggle for agency that characterizes modern life. In 1982 Great Britain retook the Falkland Islands, which had been invaded by Argentina, and this campaign turned Mrs Thatcher from the least popular prime minister the country had ever had to the most popular.

Opposition and protest may have been the way ahead, but at the time it was difficult for Derek to see his way forward. 'Every path now ran into closed doors', he wrote later. 'Everything seemed set against me, the political climate – even the weather.' He drew upon an image from alchemy to indicate himself being prepared for transformation: 'they were years of distillation; I was in the retort, screwed down'.[13] Derek was delayed with *Caravaggio* and he claims that frustration over this slow progress stoked his appetite for sexual encounters, which he preferred at this time to be casual, preferably even anonymous, therefore separated from love. He led a very active sex life. Frustrations with work fuelled his promiscuity.[14]

He continued painting, having enjoyed the activity again in relation to the B2 show, preparing for a solo exhibition at the Edward Totah gallery in November 1982. From March to May came the hectic and triumphant work in Florence, designing Ken Russell's production of Stravinsky's *The Rake's Progress*. Designer and producer agreed that Hogarth's eighteenth century should be subtly updated to twentieth-century London, with the result that Derek's design work for it joins a group of works by him that feature such freedom with questions of period: these include *The Tempest* and (when they came to be made) *Caravaggio* and *Wittgenstein*. Such a strategy can't create the contemporary relevance of the subject-matter, but it at least clarifies the realization that the importance of the ideas and themes in the works is not simply confined within the period that the works are set in. The design presents suggestions that provide audiences with additional stimulus to thought.[15]

In May he was in Rome again, being attacked and beaten by thugs, and having another look at Caravaggio's paintings while obtaining help for the script from Suso Cecchi d'Amico. Back in London, he took Italian lessons and continued painting. In September a hero, William S. Burroughs, participated in 'The Final Academy', an event staged by Genesis P. Orridge's Psychic TV, and Derek filmed the great man on Super-8.

The paintings Derek had made for his exhibition at the Edward Totah Gallery in November are based upon black paint, and Tony Peake suggests that while this shows the influence of Caravaggio it also evokes the night life which Derek liked so much.[16] The paintings that were based on alchemical symbolism and Heraclitean philosophy might have seemed remote in significance and tangential in impact. There were others, however, from this year and the following year (as Derek continued to paint) based on the human figure. In these he applied gold leaf to the canvas, painted over it in black, and then wiped away the black paint to reveal the figures (to the viewer the result feels like a revelation, although it was of course literally a formation). In *Untitled (Archer)*, the kneeling masked archer figure, brooded over by a giant head, is based on a 1950s photograph from *Physique Pictorial* that Derek reproduced in *Dancing Ledge*.[17] However, in that book no mention is made of the painting, which leaves mysterious Derek's purpose in printing it. A much larger painting from the same series, *Irresistible Grace*, shows a sick, dead or sleeping man being lowered to the ground by two male figures, one of whom is in a state of tense sexual excitement, his genitals occupying the centre of the painting. The egg of the philosophers floats in the air above, containing the seed of spiritual rebirth that will lead to the creation of gold, or wisdom. It counterbalances a skull of physical putrefaction

Irresistible Grace, 1982, oil on canvas, 137 x 183 cm.

(a necessary prelude to spiritual rebirth) in the bottom left-hand corner. The main figure is poised between these two states. To say as much is to give the painting an alchemical interpretation. We might also note that black is the starting-point for the alchemists' 'Great Work', while the creation of gold is its purpose, which gives another inflection to Derek's apparent finding of the figures by wiping away the black paint. As in other paintings of the series, streaks of blue, green and red paint modulate the effect of the black and gold. The declining figure looks quite like a self-portrait. Derek tells us in *Dancing Ledge* that one of this series was modelled on 'El Greco's *Pietà*' and this is surely it.[18] The painting he refers to is probably the *Lamentation* in the Philadelphia Museum of Art, where St John's face is close to Christ's, as if kissing him. A sacred atmosphere, then, hovers through Derek's painting by virtue of this reference and the painting's title. The 'grace' invoked may well be divine; it is also more explicitly the grace of living gay, given the prominently depicted erection and the atmosphere of peaceful swooning acceptance that suffuses the painting.

In terms of sales, the exhibition went off, as Derek ruefully wrote later, 'like a damp squib'.[19] The last work episode of 1982 came in December when Nicholas Ward-Jackson, producer of the Caravaggio project, suggested that Derek should write about his frustration over the project seeming permanently stalled as an alternative to being overwhelmed by it, and at the end of the month Derek began to write his first memoir, *Dancing Ledge*. The composition and editing of this occupied much of 1983 and it was published at the end of February 1984. What sort of a book is *Dancing Ledge*? Given Derek's way of working (his liking for collaboration) it is important to take in the fact that he managed to transform what seems like a very lonely act (the act of writing) into something collaborative, employing a young intellectual, Shaun Allen, to type up and edit the text and to help him find the right form and order for the work, which at one point also takes the opportunity to incorporate the response of an early reader whom Derek addresses as 'Paul'.[20] Derek called it an 'autobiography' in his preface to the second edition (1991).

In the book he develops the structure that also underlies two later volumes of memoirs, *Kicking the Pricks* and *Modern Nature*. In the early part of the book he recounts his early life and this leads to the development of aesthetic and social ideas in the second half of the text. This structure is in each case modified by close attention to current concerns: for example, *Dancing Ledge* begins with Derek's interpretation of Caravaggio's art. The title carries certain associations: primarily with place (as mentioned earlier, Dancing Ledge, with Tilly Whim and Winspit, was part of the Dorset coast that Derek loved, all three places being former quarries of sought-after Purbeck stone). However, we are not told this association until the very end of the book. In the meantime 'dancing' carries connotations of joyous creative expression and 'ledge' perilous connotations, perhaps suggesting the possibility of a fall on one side, cramped lack of space on the other. It is as if Derek has been given (or has carved out for himself) a perilous narrow space for his joyful creative acts to emerge on.

In the text, which is presented as an intermittent and chronologically jumbled diary, Derek's sense of humour emerges fully. The book is full of aesthetic ideas, not just about films but architecture and painting. The book provides snatched glimpses of the social history of his times and becomes a vehicle for his poetry:

> The heaven and earth are united in gold
> he combs (his hair)
> the golden rays
> (in his hands) the roses burn
> the days are long
> the wheel turns in the circle
> cooled by breezes from the four corners
> he enters (his chamber)
> the swallow has risen (in the east)
> the doors are open[21]

By the last part of the book protest is comprehensively under way. He protests against Social Realism as an aesthetic; the fetishism of technology; Pink Floyd's anti-intellectual complicity with capital; the advertising executive turned film mogul David Puttnam and

'British Film Year'; the fetishism of art ('All art is dead, especially modern art'[22]); the political Left's unhelpful attitude about homosexuality; public harassment of gay men by the police ('A gang of uniformed hoodlums . . . protecting the degenerate establishment'[23]). His protests are fast, quick-witted, exhilarating and productive of pithy memorable phrases.

However, the book is by no means all reaction. Section X, 'Dancing Ledge', may start with a rejection of Art as a fetishized commodity removed from life, but it becomes a more concentrated meditation on ways in which creativity could be put back into society. These pages indicate the great extent to which sexuality is bound into Derek's ideas on art and life. He asserts that 'sexual encounters lead to knowledge'. He argues that 'Sexuality colours my politics – I distrust all figures of authority, including the artist. Homosexuals have such a struggle to define themselves against the order of things.'[24] One friend whose figure emerges in these pages with particular strength is Andy Marshall.[25] Marshall was young; boisterous and obstreperous in his confrontations with the police. Derek met him as a nineteen-year-old in 1978 in a gay disco, bailed him out of police custody a few weeks later, and evidently admired him, not least for his uncompromising attitude towards authority. At least, admiration can be felt through the pages of *Dancing Ledge.* However, when he wrote them Derek was actively trying to promote the young man, so these pages might give a deliberately glamorous portrait of a Marshall that an acquaintance might not have been able to recognize at first sight. Derek had enlisted the help of Christopher Hobbs in a prolonged effort to try to keep Marshall out of the hands of the police, who, the two had decided, wanted to turn him into a criminal. On one level this involved another practical case of attempting to spread creative energy around: Derek bought some of the furniture Marshall made from scrap pieces of wood, and exhibited some more of Marshall's furniture together with his own paintings in his exhibition at the ICA early in

1984. On another level, it meant trying to coax Marshall 'to fight with the brain, not the fists'.[26] 'Andy has a GBH manner', Derek wrote.[27] (The initials refer to the charge of causing 'grievous bodily harm' made against people who injure, but do not kill, other people in an assault.) Later in the 1980s the relationship with Marshall became problematic as Derek himself became something of an authority figure to the other man.

Derek's own sense of political radicalism deepened during the early 1980s, when there was a great deal of talk in non-Conservative circles about the need to take 'direct political action' in support of goals and struggles. In the meantime the Conservative government could pursue direct action against anything it didn't like, as the trade union movement and the Greater London Council soon found out. Derek's radicalism was already well developed, rooted in his memories of the era when gay life was illegal and the subsequent liberalization. His radicalism was sharpened by his sympathy for the Campaign for Nuclear Disarmament, which went through a resurgence in the 1980s, and by other involvement: the years 1980 and 1981 saw his flirtation with the Workers' Revolutionary Party. This is recounted in *Dancing Ledge*, where we gather that party stalwart Vanessa Redgrave caused Derek to ride on buses to attend demonstrations, to attempt to sell the party's newspaper, and to accompany her in electioneering and attend party meetings, before detecting an improper level of commitment and dropping him. His involvement was brief, but we should take seriously his exposure to an earnest radical group in terms of what he could learn from it about political campaigning from a perspective that the mainstream of politics wanted to make marginal. In particular, this involves analysing events as products of forces that are pro-grammatic and institutional, involving large social movements, and getting beyond the level of individuals and personalities. 'I thoroughly agreed with what Vanessa was doing' he said later, 'here was an artist making a political intervention.'[28] The conversation of intellectual friends, such as Shaun Allen and (later on) Paul Bettell gave Derek encouragement and food for thought in this regard. Plunged into the doldrums by Thatcherite assaults on funding, the media, education, the Welfare State, labour, the middle class and in general anything she found too left-wing or liberal, Derek conceived that direct action promised renewal. Derek would follow his own advice to Marshall: 'win with the brain, not the fists'. He applied the term he had used of Marshall, GBH, to his own paintings.

The opening of the Totah Gallery show had been a conventional one. For his solo exhibition at the ICA in February 1984 (the eve of the miners' strike, Mrs Thatcher's final move, as it turned out, against the National Union of Mineworkers, who had traditionally been in the vanguard of working-class militancy) Derek must have reasoned that, if he wasn't going to sell any work, the opening at least could be an event.[29] Michael Clarke danced in a tutu and Doc Martens, and some neo-naturists attended in the nude. Andy Marshall's furniture was in place and Derek took some film of the event. That month the ICA mounted a series of his films and pop promos.[30]

For the exhibition Derek had prepared six large new paintings which together constitute his greatest work in painting. He named them the GBH series. They hung loose so that you could peer round to see the back. They are big: 10 × 8 ft (3 × 2.4 m), and are made of oil paint applied to an unusual surface made from sheets of newspaper glued together and backed on canvas. This support is about 2–3 mm thick. This surface gives the paintings extraordinary physical presence, because their surfaces are pitted, bowed, flexed, buckled, in short completely three-dimensional. The paint produces a dry matt surface on the moulded underlying support, and the entire effect is heavily tactile while the paintings, because of the newspaper, remain very fragile. Each of the six paintings shows a large circle painted over and around the upper centre of the surface.

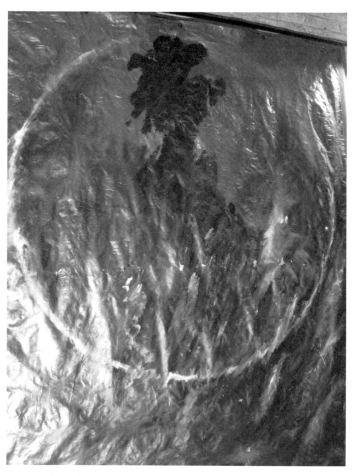

GBH (one of six paintings), 1983–4, oil on pasted sheets of newspaper backed with canvas, 10 × 8 ft (3 × 2.4 m).

GBH (detail).

In one a burnished copper disk is formed within the circle by a thin smearing of red paint over underlying gold: the defining circular border is blue, and in the corners and below it are broad short brushmarks of charcoal, white, grey and burnt sienna. The paint seems thirsty for a surface, for adhesion. The surface is rough, textured, mottled, bulging, rippling. The painting is creased, split and torn in places; it has been folded and there is now wear along the fold. It is an old, or rather, prematurely aged surface, on which some luscious clean drops of paint can be found around a central charcoal-grey stick-like pillar that occupies the middle of the painting and resembles a charred stick, or burned stump or tree.

In a second painting the surface bulges out in places, like the brittle bark of an old beech tree. The painting has a fiery bottom half. The same colours are used, without the blue. There is much more red, which surely shows the idea of burning? The central upright form is so etiolated as no longer to cohere. It is formed from red dull marks, calligraphic, dribbling, at the top half of the big O. In a section a few feet further down, below the centre, red is overpainted with black marks applied with a dry brush: the rippling of the paper surface underneath induces the effect of a flame suddenly flaring sideways in a fire.

The elephant-skin surface of a third painting is wrinkled and dried, and the painting is the darkest in the group. Black predominates. However, the artist's smearing over a brass / gold surface with charcoal paint gives a leathery effect. The idea of a map – a map of Great Britain, in fact – begins to form. The brightest part of the painting is just off what would be south-west Scotland, were this a map. Indeed, the whole surface of the painting is like the old papier-mâché relief maps of mountain ranges, cwms and oceanic trenches that used to be found in public institutions. Once the idea of a map has begun to form, the viewer notices quite distinct parts of the coast, such as The Wash. The boundary of the circle is burnished brass colour painted over the dark country.

One could be forgiven for thinking of the circles as replicating the form of an eye, and they all remind me of J.M.W. Turner's employment of the form in certain late paintings such as *The Evening of the Deluge*. However, a better explanation might be found in an equation with externalized instruments of vision. The circles induce us to focus on the particular parts of the paintings contained within them. They begin to connote a target or the targeting sights of a bombing mission. In the context of a map, though, the circles also become like the one in the Hereford *Mappa Mundi* (c. 1300) which demarcates the temporal and the timeless realms of the world. The *Mappa* suggests harmony: a chart of the moral and spiritual order of the world, forming a contrast with Derek's depiction of late twentieth-century misrule and chaos.

In a fourth painting of the six the circle is defined in white, and there is plenty of red, pale grey and blue paint drifting over northern England. There is red around the Scottish coasts, in fact towards the edges of a black Scotland. The grey, red and blue paint over England begins to resemble drifting smoke, and with this perception I realize that it is reminiscent of the aerial photograph of a bombing raid. Simultaneously, Scotland looks like the pillar of fire and smoke from an explosion seen in elevation view. The idea of a target comes home to roost. If this interpretation holds, it suggests that Derek is linking the assault on Britain of the early 1980s with his father's violence. But the violence done to the country is also more general. Here GBH is being done to GB. The Thatcher government's unleashing of enormous and destructive change throughout the country, which had already provoked rioting in inner cities, and which involved dividing the country against itself (in July 1984 Thatcher famously described striking trade unionists as 'the enemy within') is clearly implied. For Derek the map represented a shift in analysis: in an interview with Emmanuel Cooper he says that getting away from the idea that Mrs Thatcher was solely responsible for the direful situation moved him 'to a more world view, hence the map and so on'.[31]

The entire series is marked by gorgeous wonderful surfaces and glowing colours, their light and colour seeping or oozing out of the surface of the paintings. The surfaces make you want to wrap yourself in them like a skin. Can these paintings be linked to any other of Derek's works? The use of a frame within the frame is like that in *Painting A*, as is his use of dramatic, evident, exuberant brushwork. In terms of how the paint is applied, the brushwork is a complete departure from everything he had done since – the tight landscapes, the dark unbrushed paintings. The *GBH* paintings are, however, a different sort of landscape painting. In a fifth painting Britain is red. The circular line is half gold, half red. The country could be burning or just glowing warmly. Close up, the effect is of blur, of mist, an approximative coastline defined by a red gleam, except for the island of Anglesey which has some calligraphic squiggling worked with gold paint. The effect is fantastic: a gorgeous surface of colour, a bit frightening in its intensity.

In the sixth painting Great Britain is writhing to a stick-like form of smoke and ash. A patch of red pigment in the North Sea emanates from its support like part of a cave painting on a rocky wall.

These paintings could be arranged in a sequence, with the first two I described being the last two in sequence, where Britain has been reduced by fire. The country glows red, is bombed, burns, becomes a red stick glowing with fire and, surrounded by heaps of embers, ends as a charred stump. Anyone who can remember Britain before 1979 and who lived through the untold harm that the Conservative governments of 1979–97 did to the country will recognize the metaphor as entirely appropriate. An accidental tear in one painting allows one to read a fortuitous telegram, as it were, from another time. The discontinuous words from some news report read: 'still work . . . compulsion . . . any horse-trading with the Govern- . . . democracy'. A fragmented agenda from the time.

There is no reason why Derek might not have invented the form he uses in this series – a circle in a rectangle. It is not complicated or recondite. Yet it had already been employed in esoteric and mystical contexts which it is reasonable to assume that Derek knew. Two of Robert Fludd's images of creation, 'The Division of the Waters' and 'The Chaos of the Elements', show flames and smoke and a circle in a black square. Derek knew Fludd's work and wrote of basing paintings on Fludd's 'technical drawings'.[32] The other precedent is in the work of one of the poets and artists that Derek admired most, William Blake. In his prophetic book *Milton* (1804–11) Blake had published his own print of two figures against a yellow/gold circle surrounded by flames and smoke. The accompanying lines describe Los,[33] the spirit of poetic prophecy, invigorating the narrator:

William Blake, plate 21 from *Milton* (1804–11), hand-coloured relief etching.

And Los behind me stood: a terrible flaming Sun: just close
Behind my back: I turned round in terror, and behold:
Los stood in that fierce glowing fire; & he also stoop'd down
And bound my sandals on in Udan-Adan; trembling I stood
Exceedingly with fear & terror, standing in the Vale
Of Lambeth; but he kissed me and wishd me health.
And I became One Man with him arising in my strength:
Twas too late now to recede, Los had enterd into my soul;
His terrors now posses'd me whole; I arose in fury & strength.

The image of two male figures touching, one kissing and
enheartening the other, the two of them uniting as One Man,
would seem capable of arousing the interest of a later twentieth-
century queer artist/poet. If Blake and Fludd's works are at all
relevant to Derek's GBH paintings beyond a formal level, they
provide images of destruction and renewal, on one hand, and
strength and inspiration on the other.

With respect to another medium, too, it is interesting to note
that in *Kicking the Pricks* Derek tells us that one of the titles considered for the film that eventually became *The Last of England*
(1987) was GBH.[34] This betokens a congruence of themes.

6

8 Millimetre versus 35 Millimetre

Together with nine other film directors, Derek was invited in 1986 to contribute a short film based on an aria from the world of opera to a feature film the producer Don Boyd was compiling. The result, *Aria* (1987), contained contributions from Nicolas Roeg, Bruce Beresford, Jean-Luc Godard, Robert Altman, Julien Temple, Charles Sturridge, Franc Roddam, Ken Russell and Derek. While he could not be sure what the other directors were making, Derek should have had a shrewd idea that they would all abide quite slavishly to the orthodox studio or feature film method of making films: that is to say that they would shoot in 35 mm (and possibly 16 mm for external footage) with high-gloss production values, attempt to follow narratives, and in general make the films look as expensive as possible.

For his own contribution he chose the aria 'Depuis le Jour' from Gustave Charpentier's *Louise*. He shot the film in both 35 mm and Super-8. The film opens in colour: an old lady, filmed in 35 mm, bows on stage in a shower of rose-petals. She looks thoughtful but content. Intercut with this sequence are a series of scenes, some black and white and some in colour, all filmed out of doors in Super-8, of a young woman: in a garden, at the sea, frolicking in the waves with a young man. Some of the scenes are in dreamy slow-motion, others in jerky fast stop-motion (others are in normal motion). Because the frame of an 8-mm film is sixteen times smaller than the 35-mm frame, Super-8 can record a different amount of information than is recorded in 35 mm. Particularly when later blown up to 35 mm for projection in cinemas (as in this case) the focus can soften, become approximative and even look blurry. These properties make the 8-mm sections of 'Depuis le Jour' look simpler than the 35-mm. The technologies used imply the passage of time: because it looks simpler, the 8 mm footage also looks older than the rest. Combining apparent simplicity with apparent age, it looks more primitive. Its strong associations with home movies give it an added connotation of memory. So, although all the footage was shot in 1986, the viewer forms the idea that the young woman and the old woman are the same person, who, bowing out of life, is remembering being young, happy and in love many decades previously.

The result is a very beautiful and emotionally compelling five-minute film that matches the beautiful singing of the aria by Leontyne Price. It has, however, never been accorded any importance in discussions of Derek's work. This is partly because the overall film, *Aria*, has been disparaged and written off. None of the contributions by the other directors can be considered anywhere near their best work. Derek's segment stands head and shoulders above all the others. In fact, he managed a wonderful subversion in this film. The other directors not only look enslaved to a more cumbersome film-making process, the conventional feature method, but their work, striving for narrative and in some cases even making the actors mime to the singing, looks very threadbare in imaginative resources. They seem obsessed by death; the films are often violent, and only for the young. The cumulative vulgarity of conceptions and process is amazingly exposed by Derek's poignant, restrained, discreet and wholly effective imaginative conception, which is inseparable from his working method. The Super-8 camera achieves effects impossible with the cumbersome equipment, requiring gantry and track, of 35 mm. In one continuous shot we pick up and follow a seagull in

The spirit's freedom in memory: seagull in 'Depuis le Jour' from *Aria* (1986).

a relatively complicated flight above some waves breaking on a rocky shore, as the bird doubles back, sinks, then resumes its former course.[1] This sequence could not have been spontaneously captured on 35 mm, yet it adds enormously to the idea of the spirit's freedom in memory that the film creates.

'Depuis le Jour' radiates authority. By the time he made it Derek had become expert in both 8 mm and 35 mm. In October 1984 he had participated in a film-makers' trip to the Soviet Union sponsored by the British Film Institute. There he found a strange doppelgänger world: at a time when British police were being employed to attack striking coal-miners, and to raid and close gay bookshops and pubs, the forms of censorship in the Soviet Union, rather than seeming grotesquely out of place in the modern world, looked like the other side of the same coin. Derek filmed in Super-8 in Moscow and Baku, and in the house, now a museum, that had once belonged to the film director Sergei Eisenstein. He was also given footage by some of the other film-makers on the trip. Supplementing this footage on his return with video of an artist painting a group of young men in British army uniforms holding a red flag (a metaphor for the mutual dependencies of repression in East and West) in remarkably quick time Derek produced a 27-minute film, *Imagining October*. The use of a painter was not simply a further homage to Caravaggio but, as a section of Derek's memoir *Kicking the Pricks* (1987) makes clear, it fulfilled a more complicated impulse relating to the question of the use and function of art (and therefore by implication the use of the film we see it in).[2] In a terse poetry of captions that evoke the days of silent films (Eisenstein's era) Derek set out a summary protest against the present times: 'Market forces . . . audience ratings / Best means to crush Effective Expression of independent conscience'. The poetry shows the influence of Allen Ginsberg, and also of William Blake, one of whose own poems ('The Sick Rose', 1794) is reproduced in the film, and another (*Proverbs of Hell*), slightly misquoted. Condemning the age ('Crimes against genius and humanity, / History ransacked, / Promoting poverty of intellect and emotion') Derek is able to suggest some hope, on a smaller and indeed individual scale (although in retrospect it is no less important for that)

Private Solution

Sitting in Eisenstein's study
With a home movie camera
Imagining October
A cinema of small gestures

Derek is shown in Eisenstein's study, conceiving the film that the viewer is watching. The artist, it seems, after all has a place amidst the iniquities and follies of the contemporary world, pointing out hypocrisies, celebrating human energy, protesting the crimes of capital and state. Making the film is therefore itself a positive response to the depressing state of the world. The last phrase quoted above became a key term for what Derek came to think of as his own form of film-making, based in Super-8, that he was also exploring at the time through other work that became the film *The Angelic Conversation* (1985).

The film for this was taken in the summer of 1984. A Super-8 cassette normally gives 3 minutes 20 seconds of film at a speed of eighteen frames per second. However, Derek's camera allowed film to be taken at six frames per second, which would allow a cassette to last three times as long, thus easing anxiety about running out of film before the end of whatever action he desired to film, as well as making the process considerably cheaper. Projected at a speed of three frames per second onto the wall, the ten-minute cassette stretched to twenty minutes. The result was recorded on VHS videotape for editing before being transferred and blown up onto 35-mm film. The result for the viewer is akin to watching a series of very rapidly flashed still photographs. They coalesce into a moving picture, but one never loses the effect of a series of individual moments. Time slows. Small on-camera movements take on enormous presence. A flickering candle-flame appears to have a paper-like texture, as it shows the circular cells that constitute 8-mm film. The aesthetic effect thus relies heavily on the physical manipulation of the materiality of the image. Instead of taking for granted the transparency of the support, like an orthodox 35-mm film-maker, Derek explores and experiments with the matter of film, producing slow and unusual effects.

The Angelic Conversation has no narrative in its 78-minute length. Instead it presents a series of sequences that have symbolic or psychic themes: a journey; ordeals; conflict with oneself; homage and service paid to a king; the underworld; a garden of the memory of love. Derek claimed the whole to be Jungian, even in method, since he shot the film first and then decided what the thematic

Out of the underworld: *The Angelic Conversation* (1985), 8-mm film.

groupings could be afterwards. This is presumably what he meant when he wrote that reading Jung had given him the confidence to let his dream images drift and collide together.[3] The result is his personal favourite among his films: enigmatic but gentle and lyrical. He described it as 'not narrative, it's poetry'.[4] The film's central theme is gay love, enhanced as a theme by a soundtrack featuring Judi Dench reading sonnets by William Shakespeare, chosen by Derek for the tough-mindedness of their exploration of the psychology of love. Derek wrote that using Dench avoided allowing the audience to think that one of the two male characters was speaking the poems and thus introducing an idea of hierarchy. The female voice also distances and generalizes gay love, which simply becomes love, without a need for the qualifying adjective.

The Angelic Conversation premiered at the Berlin Film Festival in February 1985, and in Britain that summer. *Imagining October* was never really shown, apparently because Berlin film authorities felt that it would jeopardize the safety of the Soviet citizens who had allowed Derek to film them. The producer, James Mackay, believes that the suppression of *Imagining October* helped to motivate Derek to undertake *The Last of England*, in which the themes of the earlier film are taken up and developed differently.[5] Nevertheless, by the summer of 1985 Derek was building up a head of steam in 8-mm film-making, pushing new techniques beyond the point that he had reached in *In the Shadow of the Sun*. He would film on impulse and without scripts, composing the films afterwards out of the available material, completely separating soundtrack from image-track, doing everything differently from orthodox feature-film making, even finding a phrase, 'a cinema of small gestures', in which to claim this film-making for himself. Yet this was just when *Caravaggio* finally went into production, which meant beginning filming in September that year in orthodox fashion in 35 mm for the first time. The script had received seventeen rewrites (thirteen of them by Derek) and he had just devoted a lot of intense energy to a completely different form of film-making. He had been taking pride in evolving a form of cinema with no narrative. He loathed scripts and had made two films without them. Yet here he was committing to a project about a painter of whom next to nothing is known beyond that his life was violent and (more ambiguously) he might have been bisexual or even gay. Into this life Suso Cecchi d'Amico, the veteran Italian scriptwriter, had attempted to inject some narrative, as *Dancing Ledge* shows us.

While *Caravaggio* remains Derek's best-known film simply because it was the best promoted, it is not his finest film. The first twenty minutes have pace and life, and in particular the scene in which a scrawny Dexter Fletcher as young Caravaggio whirls round and round with a bottle, tormenting and driving off a suited 'art-lover', both of them flushed pink with exertion in a pale jade room, is very memorable. After that an ebbing of energy is perceptible. Writing at the time in the *New Statesman*, Adam

Mars-Jones identified a reason, arguing that Dexter Fletcher realized an 'extreme temperament . . . amoral and almost alarmingly alive', while Nigel Terry playing 'the mature Caravaggio has lost all that dynamism', seeming more melancholy than anything.[6]

At one moment in the film Caravaggio himself reiterates Derek's argument that 'art is theft', and at another exults in having trapped 'pure spirit in matter', immediately lamenting however that what should be 'free as the lilies in the field is perverted and hangs over the altars of Rome'. What might be termed the ideological dilemma, whereby the artist is bought exclusively by the rich and powerful just as he in turn buys his models, is an interesting central theme in the film. In *Dancing Ledge* Derek had written, 'The spurious individualism of the Renaissance, which both engendered and was born of capital, is dying. An art which began by collaborating with the banks of the Medici ends in bankruptcy on Wall St.'[7] Derek makes a point in the film about class conflict that has never been properly registered: the people who die because of their entanglement with the Renaissance art milieu are the working-class couple, Lena and Ranuccio.

In the book that accompanied the film Derek made the point that he was 'obsessed' by the interpretation of the past.[8] Not only the past, then, but the present's uses of the past constituted his interest. Applying that to his own film explains his tendency to make comments about the present in the context of discussion of the past, as in the paragraph above.[9] The system that Derek was opposing in *Dancing Ledge* was larger than specific individuals, but the activities of a relatively few people in the mid-1980s encapsulated it for him. Looking about, he could see the Saatchi brothers intervening heavily in the contemporary art market while, through their advertising agency, ensuring that their clients Mrs Thatcher and the Conservative Party were elected and re-elected. Meanwhile a Saatchi crony, the advertising man David Puttnam, became a film producer and had been heavily involved in British Film Year.

Puttnam's production *Chariots of Fire* was featured at Cannes in 1981 and Derek discovered that Puttnam had told actor Ian Charleson to claim it as his first film, when in fact Charleson had had a prominent role in *Jubilee*.[10] Charleson apologized to Derek, but here was a rewriting of history by the advertising man that smacked of the totalitarian states east of the Iron Curtain and fed some of the ironies underlying *Imagining October*. After that Derek the ant frequently criticized Puttnam the giant in public, and Puttnam was not above trying to crush his adversary with sarcasm.[11] In the activities of the Saatchis and Puttnam, Derek found a nexus embracing wealth and class interest, politics, art and cinema, some of the subject-matter of *Caravaggio*.

Critical responses to *Caravaggio* were divided. The 'dreary' film that 'fails to excite' and has a 'coldness about it' found by *City Limits* has to be set against the *Financial Times*' opinion that the film's 'guiding star' is 'Caravaggio's quest for truth' which makes the film mesmeric.[12] However, among the critics enthusiasts certainly outnumbered curmudgeons. The interesting pattern from the present perspective is that the more popular and down-market the publication the more greatly the critics seemed to relish the film. An honourable exception to this was provided by no less a figure than the eminent painter and art historian Sir Lawrence Gowing, who reviewed the film for the *Times Literary Supplement*. Gowing found the film to be 'a rather remarkable meditation' derived from Caravaggio's pictures and his times, 'an interesting and original reverie on the subject of the re-imagining of the past . . . [it has] undoubted beauty and sometimes [offers] quite useful bases for speculation about how the pictures came to be painted'. Turning his attention to the sexuality, he states: 'I do not know that the poetry of manual release has been better filmed.'[13] Here he seems to be alluding to a voice-over in which the dying Caravaggio remembers from his boyhood an early sexual moment with Pasqualone:

I watch the ripples in his trousers. 'Can I put my hand in?'
The words fall over themselves with embarrassment . . . I kneel
beside him and reach timidly into the dark . . . His cock grows
warm in my hand. Pasqualone says his girl Cecilia holds it
harder. 'Harder, Michele!'

In his interview with *Square Peg* Derek had said that 'the Pasqualone
story, that is my story. The voice-overs on the deathbed are directly
autobiographical.'[14] However, the only hands in pockets anecdotes
he tells in the memoirs are not set in Italy when he was four but
later in an RAF base in Abingdon. They concern the airman Johnno
and are dated in *At Your Own Risk* to the 1950s.[15]

Not many other critics referred so directly as Gowing to the
description of sex. In *Newsweek* Edward Behr, finding the film to be
both 'bold and quirky' and 'chaste, poetic and restrained' reassures
readers that the film is 'about 100 times more tasteful than what
millions of 10-year-olds watch on television every night'.[16] Dilys
Powell, writing for *Punch*, found the faces hypnotic:

Darkly moving . . . [the film] sends one away reluctant to
look at another film that day . . . brooding, savage . . . rich
to the eye . . . It is the faces one sees, intense, depraved and
painterly, lecherous, mocking and beautiful . . . Derek Jarman
has captured . . . what he persuades one is the sense of a law-
less, violent underground society. The action is well played.
Nevertheless, it is the faces which communicate. To have
found in today's world such incarnation of the past is itself
a triumph.[17]

This seems to have been a triumph for Derek's 'cinema of small
gestures'. In an interview he said of the film's quiet periods, 'I've
concentrated in *Caravaggio* on small gestures – little things like
the flicker of an eye . . . the tear on a cheek.'[18] The implication is

Caravaggio (1986).

of lessons learned from 8 mm applied to the different form of 35 mm. But plangent faces are a feature of Caravaggio's art.

There is always more, in Caravaggio's paintings, than an immaculate finish able to communicate a realism so entrancing that it looks lovingly painted. The extra element is a poignant psychological or spiritual life in the characters. Thus in the paintings of St Matthew, the apostle who has to write his gospel seems unused to writing, and crouches over his desk as if it were a workbench. He has to be reminded of what he wanted to say by an angel sent down for the purpose by a kindly god. In *Rest on the Flight into Egypt* an angel has been sent down to help the holy family. The angel plays the violin to lull the Virgin and Child to sleep, but he doesn't know the music off by heart, so Joseph obligingly holds up the music for him (and us) to read. Joseph's expression is concentrating, serious, a little tired and sceptical. In another painting, as St Peter is nailed to his cross he strains upwards to study the work of nailing, as if his main concern is the workmanlike one that it should be well done. This element of his subject's painting Derek conveys perfectly, first in an early shot of the mother of the dumb Gerusalemme standing still and weeping silently as her son leaves to take up his life as Caravaggio's assistant, and later near the end when a man engaged in a deposition scene looks steadily into the camera. A non-professional actor and actress were used and in both cases the shot is held for several seconds while a plangent humanity is apparent.

The film is visually impressive, influenced by the appearance of Italian neo-realism, and the production design by Christopher Hobbs, the costumes by Sandy Powell and Gabriel Beristain's cinematography, which was rewarded with a prize at the Berlin Film Festival, cannot be faulted. The film also attracted talented actors, giving Tilda Swinton her first film role, for example, and relying heavily on the excellent performance of Sean Bean. If there is a problem it lies with the script, tortured through its rewrites, as several critics pointed out at the time.[19] People rarely talk to each other in this film. The usual mode is that a character makes a statement which is met with silence. The central bisexual triangle (Lena, Ranuccio, Caravaggio) persuaded critics, however. For Mark Finch they were 'grubby in desperation and sly in the knowledge of desire and its immutability'.[20] 'Its passion communicates blazingly' wrote Mark Castell in the *Sunday Telegraph*, taking the painterly and poetic qualities together with the bisexual triangle to consti-tute 'a stimulating and sometimes mischievously funny debate on sexuality and social mores, art and politics'.[21]

While not his best film, and not winning any other awards, it was important that *Caravaggio* finally got made, since it gave Derek credibility. 'Director's Triumph as Scholar and Visionary' was the headline of the article in *The Times*.[22] He had pushed through the big project, which proved a very interesting and worthwhile one, and accrued some kudos and lustre as a result. For the *Mail on Sunday*, 'braving the flak of a recent attack by Tory MP Winston

Churchill, the startling talent of Derek Jarman advances in triumph – to the front rank of British film-makers'.[23] Nevertheless, Derek felt constrained by the elaborate demands of 35 mm, where every shot has to be carefully calculated and set up in elaborate consultations with camera, sound operator, focus puller, stand ins and so on. Derek's immediate response after *Caravaggio* was to return to unfinished business with Super-8.[24]

A return to Super-8 meant a return to a different group of collaborators, especially to a group of men some of whom had recently graduated from film school, and in some combination worked on all of Derek's 8-mm and music video in the 1980s – Richard Heslop, Christopher Hughes, Cerith Wyn Evans, Peter Cartwright and a different producer, James Mackay (producer of *The Angelic Conversation* and *Imagining October*). Filming was done during several months of 1986 for a project that Derek was forming under a series of working titles: GBH and *Three Minutes to Midnight* connect this project to the ICA painting retrospective of 1984 when the GBH series was shown in a space shared by some of Andy Marshall's longcase clocks, stopped with that time on their dials. *The Dead Sea* seemed to fit less well as a name and eventually *The Last of England* was preferred. Ford Madox Brown's painting of that name shows emigrants beginning an exile from home in the 1850s: asked in an interview with *Marxism Today* about the relevance of this, Derek said 'I'm a complete exile in my own country.'[25]

The occasional, spontaneous 8-mm filming for the project was undertaken out and about in various locations (including unlucky New York, where Derek went for *Caravaggio*'s opening and lost his lover of the moment, called Spring, who features in the early parts of *The Last of England*). It was supplemented by a week-long production shoot in the deserted Royal Victoria Docks, East London. The location had been rented to film pop promos by The Smiths and Easterhouse; but after they were done, time still remained for shooting Derek's first film. Derek thus had footage, made without a script and for next to nothing (in film terms). The expensive part of the process, which eventually took most of the film's budget of £260,000, was post-production: selecting and assembling the desired footage, transferring to video to add colour and to achieve the extremely fast editing that the film exhibits, which was only possible on video,[26] and then transferring and blowing up to 35-mm film. The artistic success of the final film owes a great deal to the sound track made by Simon Fisher Turner and to Nigel Terry's delivery of the four voice-overs Derek wrote for the film. Derek wrote that the film 'works with image and sound, a language which is nearer to poetry than prose'.[27] With the single exception of a parody of a Remembrance Day ceremony the image track and the sound track are entirely separate systems. The normal and entirely tedious cinematic conventions of shot / reverse shot, 180 degree rule, eye-line shot and establishing shot are entirely absent, together with story, plot, bridging shots and crane shots. The resulting film contains lengthy sequences in which the camera wanders amongst a group of people, filming an event or action that seems to exist outside the film-world itself. The hand-held cameras sway about as people walk, and weave in and out of groups. The event seems bigger than the film and camera, which appear to have found it and to be witnessing it, rather than everything simply looking, as in a conventional film, as if it has been staged for the film. As such these sequences clearly pre-figure much of the 'reality' style camera-work of twenty-first-century British and international television and film. When, for example, the director Nicholas Hytner expressed pleasure in being able to use two hand-held cameras during the filming of a scene in *The History Boys* so that the cameras seemed to become part of the action, he was, consciously or not, following Derek's example.[28]

Tilda Swinton uses the phrase 'pre-industrial' to describe the film-making for *The Last of England*.[29] The point was to make a commercial film and then be able to take a completed product to

Tilda Swinton with Spencer Leigh's hand in *The Last of England* (1987).

distributors, rather than obtain their money at the beginning and have to start compromising.

The result is completely unlike any other feature film. It fills in the detail of the vision of Britain as bombed and abused that was worked through on a large scale in the GBH painting series. The continual fires and smoke in the film establish continuity with the paintings on the basic level of this imagery. Robert Hewison describes the film's strangeness:

> There is no narrative . . . There is no dialogue. At most there is a situation, evoked by sounds and images that are constantly running into one another, across each other, against each other . . . Jarman offers an artist's vision in place of the conventional naturalistic fictions of an orthodox film maker.[30]

Hewison is interested in the social position of art, and his discussion of the film emphasizes that. In fact, despite his assertion, there are eight lines of dialogue in the film, all of it occurring during the

parody of the Remembrance Day ceremony. An actress playing a
Royal speaks to an actor playing a masked soldier:

Is it loaded?
Yes ma'am.
Did you enjoy the Falklands?
Yes, ma'am.
Preparing for the next one then?
Yes, ma'am.
(*with relish*) It's going to be the big one, isn't it?
Hope so, ma'am.

The exchange links the militaristic oppression visible in the film
with the Falklands campaign of 1982, and the dangerous possibility
of other petty-imperial adventures. Here Derek seems to have been
a prophet.

Michael O'Pray concludes that *The Last of England* is 'Jarman's
most brilliant film, a major artistic achievement . . . One of the key
British films of the '80s, if not of the post-war period . . . carries
Jarman's critique of British post-imperialism to its furthest point.'[31]
Other commentators add different interpretations. Annette Kuhn
is interested in personal memory, and her view over-emphasizes
a mournful and melancholy element in the film, despite an elated
response being recognizable in some of her phrases. For her the
film is a 'stunning array of sounds and images . . . [which] pile up
on each other. The vision is kaleidoscopic . . . this hallucinating
dream . . . this dazzling display has . . . a compelling, desperate
beauty.'[32] Gus Van Sant has put on record his own technical debt
to the film (and to the promos for The Smiths and The Pet Shop
Boys): 'There are things you do with a Super-8 camera that you
don't do with a bigger one.'[33] However, for the artistic effect of
the film, Will Self's summation is the best: 'in *The Last of England*
[Jarman] offered us a set of discursive and yet plangent images of

our own divided nature: its beauty and brutality, its sensuality and its darkness'.[34]

Whatever else it may be, *The Last of England* is a wholesale attack on Thatcherite ideology. The sequence showing the naked, weeping, distraught man who is unable to feed himself adequately intercut with film of another man, weak in himself and held together by a series of calipers, yet wasting the world's resources, is the pithy heart of an economic protest, just as other parts of the film demonstrate Derek's protests at other aspects of the Thatcherite nightmare. Government misrule becomes a main factor in the break-up of the natural world and the social order. The 'Land of Hope and Glory' sequence is bitterly ironic, as is the parody of a royal wedding. Nigel Terry's four voice-overs set up the film's vision by delivering Derek's rough and ready poetry ('The oaks died this year. On every green hill mourners stand, and weep for the last of England'). Terry's voice gives a dry and forceful delivery stressing the anger and irony of the poetry and downplaying its melancholy and sorrow.[35] *The Last of England* is an angry film, and Derek told radio listeners a few years later that 'anger fuelled my work . . . a lot of my films', particularly anger at the political situation. One of the poems in the film explicitly invokes two earlier poems that contributed to the film-maker's vision, by quoting from Allen Ginsberg's *Howl*, 'I saw the best minds of my generation destroyed by madness / Starving hysterical naked' and from T. S. Eliot's *The Waste Land*. The dystopia of *The Last of England* is a late-century development from Eliot. In Derek's working notebooks for the film, phrases such as 'the crowds flowing over London Bridge' and 'Time Present Time Past Time Future' are strongly evocative of Eliot's *The Waste Land* and *Four Quartets*. They indicate that the earlier poet's energies were active in Derek's imagination.[36] Derek described the film as a 'dream allegory': 'in dream allegory the poet wakes in a visionary landscape where he encounters personifications of psychic states'.[37] Here he implicitly acknowledges his debt to his first degree at King's College: the most famous dream allegory is probably the medieval poem *Piers Plowman* by John Langland – rarely read, I suggest, except on university literature courses.

The notebook in which Derek quotes Eliot also shows how he developed a metaphor between the poetic voice-overs and the imagery of the film. One voice-over tells us that 'Citizens stood mute watching children devoured in their prams' before 'the Dinosaurs' moved on. The notebook refers to a filmed sequence (which became part of the final film) of a baby in a pram full of the gutter press, and 'an image of the child fucked up in copies of The Sun'. The form that the predation (and the dinosaurs) can take is thus revealed. Derek wrote next 'These images speak for themselves strong clear montage.'

He was also careful to note exact thoughts about particular sequences: 'Use the sequence of Spring jacking up as in the rushes virtually unedited so that the image is reinforced by constant repetition. Sound. Real sound. No music and a heart beat and gasping for breath.' Later, 'Spring smashing the Profane Love. Again this sequence . . . must look like the rushes.'[38] All this is very faithfully in the final film. It is difficult to envisage a studio-bound orthodox feature film director even being able to think this way.

Derek's notebooks for *The Last of England* present a fascinating spectacle of the film-maker's poetry at work. Large, like fat photograph albums, and seemingly written as continuous wholes rather than being subdivided into different organizational parts, the books show the film-maker's ideas appearing, evolving, developing and being cut back. Towards the beginning of the first notebook, for example, the film is envisaged as a series of tales told by a spider in a bell jar.[39] A version of the Emperor Hirohito voice-over occurs amidst intense brooding on William Blake and on Matthew Arnold's 'Dover Beach'. In all the early different drafts, which merge almost seamlessly into each other, fragments of what became the final voice-overs can be made out. It is remarkable how Derek managed to pick the good parts out of the rest of the abandoned paragraphs, sentences and passages. Specific and dated references disappear: 'In the plutonium secrecy of the English suburb', becomes 'in the silence of an English suburb' in the final film. 'The bureaucrat from the Ministry poisoned the last buttercup in Langton last week' becomes 'nothing but a bureaucrat from the Ministry poisoning the buttercups'. The specific reference that disappears in the final version is surely to the village of Langton Matravers in Derek's beloved Dorset. Also in the notebooks are establishing notes to himself: at the beginning, 'May 1986 after the nuclear accident the more formal film seems to be essentially obsolete. The situation changes since January we've had the Libya raid and the Soviet accident.' Towards the middle of the notebook, where the ideas have been renamed '3 Minutes to Midnight' comes a meditation on the nature of film:

> Can this melancholy with its inactivity become the film / film which [word obliterated] projects the others fiction adopting adapting can this film so dependent on the violence of narrative. The cut. The true cut. The final cut make present a sunset these flowers the difficulty of being is the difficulty of being in . . .

At this point in the notebook he begins repeating and rewriting the earlier poems. All these extensive written notes are interpersed with pasted-in postcards painted black by Derek, bearing in gold ink his handwritten notes for visual images: 'Tilda at Kimmerhame', for example, 'Introduce low shots of Pavements etc.', 'Two boys smoking blow-backs. Better than above scene.' 'Tilda and the English Rose.' 'Naked boy on a horse.' The next notebook's similar note 'Perhaps the shot of rain in a puddle' reminds us that the Dutch silent-film director Joris Ivens is mentioned admiringly several times in *Modern Nature* yet never cited in the literature on Jarman as an influence.

The point to emphasize, however, is that in the notebooks poetic words and specific images are planned and placed together. The meditative subjective poet's notebook has replaced the orthodox script as a vehicle for creative work.

The film is exhilarating though its vision is bleak, and Derek was careful to quote Colin McCabe and Tilda Swinton to that effect in *Kicking the Pricks*.[40] The exhilaration comes from the film's unprecedented aesthetic success. Here is something new as a feature film. Just as his 'cinema of small gestures' of *Imagining October* and *The Angelic Conversation* went beyond the place he had reached in his 1970s 8-mm work, so *The Last of England*'s reliance on superfast video editing means that it goes beyond the point reached in any of the earlier films. It also recapitulates the earlier techniques, filming directly into sunlight or strong artificial light to induce the film to turn black, for example, as Derek had done in the early 1970s, and using cinema of small gestures when Tilda Swinton arrives in the later stages of the film. It therefore amounts to a monument to the film-making that Derek had claimed as his own form of cinema.

Some relief from the bleakness of the themes comes from Derek's use of his grandfather Puttock's home movie footage and his father's footage showing Derek himself, at various ages starting at between one and two, scampering happily around various gardens. These few gentle lyrical moments give viewers something that we're hungry for – a feeling of delight in an otherwise uncompromising film. The childhood gardens function by contrast with an awful contemporary wasteland, where no gardens are visible. Derek's feeling of how bad life can be made, and his condemnation of the people responsible for messing up our lives (all of which come over most powerfully in *The Last of England*), hinges upon his sense of how good life can be, represented within the film by these home movies. We could say that they stand for the promise that is always made by the parents to the child – always made and never kept

– that life is as good, as safe and as happy as the best days of childhood. But on another level, Derek stated that the family's home movies 'Held [the film] together' so that thematic avenues could be explored even if they proved to be cul-de-sacs, because he could cut back to some of the home movie footage.[41] Rephrasing this in rhetorical terms gives a different angle on his working method: the presence of this found footage in the film and its relationship with the whole work represents an *anamnestic paradiegesis* – that is, a recalling of past facts that leads to further observations. (So the home movie footage is a real memory, and it leads to further thoughts and feelings that Derek provides in his own Super-8 work that constitutes the rest of the film.) In other words the themes of the film are going to be explored beside (that is, apart from) narrative: they are explored in some other way, as meditations sometimes prompted by the home movies which offer an opportunity to restart. Derek had found a way to create an art that combined his own life and his imaginative grasp of his theme. This solution is figured at the beginning of the film when we see him working in Phoenix House in the early hours, accompanied by the first poetic voice-over. This footage explicitly signifies *The Last of England* to be an example of what Derek called for in *Kicking the Pricks*: 'a cinema which grows up and uses the direct experience of the author like any other art form, and which stands up to the commissioning bodies and declares that experience is the basis for serious work'.[42] The film won two prizes at the Berlin Film Festival and another at the Madrid Film Festival. It was generally well received at the Edinburgh Film Festival and in Japan, where Derek attended the opening, less so in London and (of course) New York.

7

1986 and After

Lawrence Gowing had noted that in Derek's film Caravaggio wore 'a Wyndham Lewis hat'. In an interview in 1986 Derek said 'I'm pursued by the Left and Right, like Wyndham Lewis. I can't do anything correctly.' He also said, 'making Caravaggio exhausted me emotionally and mentally . . . I see myself at this stage as essentially having failed as a film-maker.'[1] He had every reason to feel worn out by early 1987. On a personal and emotional level 1986 had been a difficult year.

In December 1985 Derek found himself attacked by right-wing Christianist Mary Whitehouse, via her Film and Television Viewers and Listeners Association, and the Conservative Member of Parliament Winston Spencer-Churchill, with the controversy spreading well into 1986. Channel Four belatedly screened Derek's three feature films from the 1970s, having bought the rights two years earlier. Since *Jubilee*'s original release, the policies of the Conservative government had caused extensive rioting in British inner cities. A few weeks before its screening on Channel Four a young policeman was cruelly killed by a mob in a riot at a housing estate known as Broadwater Farm. *Jubilee* was therefore prophetic, but the confused right wing seemed to regard it as an incitement. Churchill's parliamentary bill to censor 'video nasties' – the pornography of violence – tried to catch Derek's films in its net and an attempt was made to extend its scope to the censorship of television, ostensibly to prevent screenings such as those of

Jubilee and *Sebastiane*. The inclusion of *Sebastiane* suggests that it wasn't the violence of the films that inflamed the right so much as the gay life and activity in the films. It has been said of Whitehouse that 'her fear of homosexuals was visceral'.[2] Whitehouse described the possibility that 'gay' might 'appear normal' as a 'new and terrible threat'.[3] She wrote asking the Director of Public Prosecutions to bring a court case against the Independent Broadcasting Authority for allowing Channel Four to broadcast Derek's films.[4] Her letter (2 December 1985) states 'It is surely a sad commentary on the state of television in Britain today.'[5] The sour critic Baglione, in *Caravaggio*, finishes typing his hostile review of the painter's work with the phrase 'A sad commentary on the state of painting today.' It is interesting that even when *Sebastiane* had first appeared in October 1976, film critics for the *Guardian* and the *Observer* newspapers were already mentioning Mrs Whitehouse's name in their reviews (presumably light-heartedly).[6] In general, however, the reception of both films' general release had been completely different from the hysteria whipped up in the mid-1980s.

Derek blamed Channel Four for not showing his films earlier. The Right blamed it for showing them at all. Caught in the middle was Channel Four's chief executive, Jeremy Isaacs. When 'film director' Michael Winner shrieked that Derek was making 'pornography', Isaacs replied that he thought Derek was 'a genius'.[7] In April Derek found himself gratuitously attacked by television 'personality' Michael Parkinson (whom Derek described mildly enough the next day as 'an old man who's out of touch'[8]). The lack of boundary between negative criticism of the works and *ad hominem* attacks was disturbing, but perhaps inevitable because so few of the attackers seemed to have watched the films. In 1987 Mrs Whitehouse was awarded a CBE by the Queen. It was said that Mrs Thatcher admired her personally.

Controversy over this issue was succeeded by further controversies directly about the representation of gay life and its status in law.

Derek defended himself in live public debates as best he could, but the experience could be rough. In a discussion in January 1988 his name was used as a definition of the word 'filth' by an audience member, probably one of Whitehouse's organization.[9] An attempted discussion with MP Gerald Howarth degenerated into an argument after Derek's shout of 'Rubbish! Absolute rubbish!' drew out Howarth's ill-concealed homophobia ('You disgust me').[10] The encounter left Derek stunned and (temporarily) lost for words.

In the autumn of 1986 Derek's father Lance died after suffering several strokes. At his bedside, understanding that his father, though he could not speak, could probably hear, Derek felt that he should speak to him, but could not do so. His father and he had never developed a way of communicating feelings, and he felt that at Lance's deathbed it was 'too late to invent one'.[11] Thinking back on his parents a few years later, Derek shows his extraordinary honesty:

How should I recall them? The relief I felt when they were gone, buried, and could no longer pry? That they remained like an echo in the silence of my privacy, though long dead? I could write of them with sympathy, forget to tell you that my heart danced on their last breath.[12]

Lance Jarman had left Derek enough money to pay for the lease-hold of the flat in Phoenix House, and to secure a sanctuary, in the form of Prospect Cottage, Dungeness, which he found and acquired in May 1987. The nuclear power station is just a mile and a half from the cottage (but looks closer because of its vast size). Derek's attitude to this presence changed over the years. In the notebook for *The Last of England* there is a postcard with Derek's handwriting in gold (therefore a note for a shot in the film): 'The brooding black of the Dungeoness B'.[13] The punning misspelling of the name reflects a dislike and mistrust of the British nuclear industry shared by many people at the time.[14] Later, after moving to Dungeness, and without changing his mind about the secretive shenanigans of the industry, Derek came to appreciate the sheer bulk and array of lights on the buildings, gleaming at night like a vast ocean liner.[15] The reactor also had its volcanic moments, rumbling, blaring and attracting lightning-strikes in the landscape beyond the garden, yet conceptually as well as visually embraced by the garden.[16]

Derek had himself tested for the human immuno-deficiency virus and was given the results four days before Christmas 1986. The news was bad. A prospect of mortality yawned, in fairly short order since in the 1980s survival after diagnosis was of short duration. He had to assume that only a few years remained to him, but how many, and in what circumstances, were issues beyond prediction.

Stress of a more bracing and happier kind, yet stress nevertheless, surrounded the arrival in Derek's life at almost this very moment of the man whom he described, in the last words he ever wrote, as his 'true love': Keith Collins.[17] Finding that he had caught the virus, and immediately having to accommodate that knowledge with his new-found romantic interest was perhaps a major reason why Derek felt 'exhausted' by the spring of 1987. Derek found Collins (a young man of 22) to be extraordinarily loyal, loving and gentle, with a very lively sense of humour.[18] Collins also had a keen aspiration to experience social acceptance for gay men. The two men found a way of living together, managing not to be forced apart by Derek's illness.

What were Derek's attitudes to love, friendship and sex, and how did the advent of Collins affect them? On 10 January 1983 he had written in a notebook, 'I have separated sex from friendship. Friendship is undying, you live free as equals. Sex which is unimportant as long as it is plentiful, you find elsewhere. The easier this is made the more balanced life becomes.'[19] By January 1988, after a long talk of two hours with Tilda Swinton about emotional entanglements, he attempts to confirm this view: 'love for me is folly . . . I'd go for friendship any day, as for sex it's best anonymous.'[20] Things were not to prove so straightforward, however. The same winter of 1987–8 he wrote an extremely honest journal entry about the relationship with Collins and the effect of HIV on himself (which included impotence, and emotional distancing from Collins). He continues, 'In my strange way I'm in love with both Keith and Tilda though love perhaps is not the right word.'[21] The remainder of the paragraph is all about Collins. From the time of Collins' arrival the word 'love' occurs increasingly frequently in Derek's writings, with special emphasis at the end of *At Your Own Risk* and *Smiling in Slow Motion*.

Derek was also, though, engaged in a great deal of work in 1986–7: on *The Last of England*, and 'Depuis le Jour' for *Aria*; on the pop promos for The Smiths (covering four songs altogether) and others for Easterhouse (two) and Matt Fretton, The Mighty Lemon Drops, Bob Geldof (two) and The Pet Shop Boys (two). He helped prepare the volume that accompanied *Caravaggio*, including his notes on the production, and he wrote *Kicking the Pricks*. He also painted nine paintings entitled *The Caravaggio Suite* when he was nominated for the Turner Prize at the Tate Gallery in 1986, and many more works for an exhibition at Richard Salmon's in 1987. So there were good reasons for feeling worn out.

The five years between the Edward Totah exhibition at the end of 1982 and the end of 1987 were a time of explosive creativity for Derek. They saw two commercial feature films and two other Super-8 films (one feature-length); his GBH series and his 'dark' and 'broken-glass' series of paintings; important pop promos, and his first prose memoirs, a form that he proved able to use brilliantly in *Dancing Ledge* and *Kicking the Pricks*. Despite private disaster and public vilification, his art (in all its forms) emerged full of dynamism and revolutionary energies.

Kicking the Pricks is, among other things, a sustained polemic: against the film industry, and also against social and political disorder emanating from the higher levels of society and politics to trickle downwards. Yet it is far from a rant: it contains fantasies (the fantasy of shooting an un-named David Puttnam by firing squad, and that of meeting Mrs Thatcher at a Hunt Ball in Grantham and becoming Minister of Horticulture), poems, and upbringing, a concluding unacknowledged thought from Heraclitus, 'It's hard to fight against passion, for whatever it wants it buys at the expense of soul' and a liberal scattering of photographs exemplifying a range of strategies for drawing word and image into relationship. The book concentrates on Derek's Super-8 films and contains discussions of *Imagining October*, *The Angelic Conversation* and *The Last of England*. It constitutes a central statement about his views of the possibilities and practices of cinema. The book presents and argues for an aesthetics based in 8 mm, and contributes some social–historical ramifications for that aesthetics. Continuing his collaborative drive, the book contains lengthy sections presented in the form of interviews or conversations:

You were talking about why you don't miss being promiscuous.
I wasn't, you were telling me why I shouldn't miss being promiscuous.[22]

By using a flexible form combining notes from the editing room with reminiscences of his parents and the elements specified above, Derek conveys the immediacy of lived experience in the embattled circumstances of 1987; how the individual creative artist arises from and constantly interacts with his time. The form of the book is one that seems to emerge only from the demands of its internal logic and the progression of its themes. It conforms to no conventional pattern in autobiography, diary or memoir, and is thus new, fresh, like the film, *The Last of England*, that it accompanied.

The book also alludes to paintings that Derek was making at the time that incorporated smashed glass. These are relatively small works, many of which incorporate other found objects as well. Such objects adhere to a thick paste of black paint. In most cases, words have been etched or scratched on the glass in Derek's handwriting, and remain legible. One work consists of the black paint, an attached starfish towards the top right, and words forming (very approximately) the following pattern:

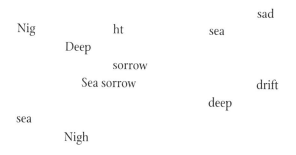

The result begins to resemble a concrete poem, where the spatial disposition of the words gives an immediate visual impact and thus contributes to the possible meanings of the poem. In these works of Derek's the glass, pushed into the paint, tends to have flattened the waves of paint beneath it into an even matt zone, so that the works contain three areas: black paint in ripples, the area of glass/flattened paint over which words are distributed, and the area filled by whatever object is incorporated. With its words, the area of flat paint/glass begins to feel like a space of thought or contemplation, spreading in a context (or even across a landscape). Another such work makes use of a small bottle in which has been placed a miniature cross surrounded by matches that look like votive candles. This bottle is stuck on its side, as if toppled. There are bullets in the paint and the shells of razor clams. Words appear in this pattern:

On the waters

```
S                                                          DEAD

                    SINKI

        MAYDA

                          SEA                    FUCK

HI         AFB                      DEAD

  DRO                                              SOS

        WNING                          MES

                                        AGE

                              NG  RE

                              BURN

    SOS                                        NO HOPE

MESSAGE           SOS

  SOS           INKING

  DEAD          F     K                              SO
```

In this case it is difficult for the viewer to find or make out all the
letters. Fragmentary words feel like 'static' on radio waves. Taken
together with its consistently three-dimensional visual elements,
this seems to be a poem about having caught the virus. Derek has
never been proposed as a concrete poet before, yet he was a friend
of the very eminent Dom Sylvester Houédard, the world's foremost
typewriter poet, whose thirst for concretion is patently visible in
letters to Derek about *Sebastiane* and *Caravaggio*, parts of which are
typewritten as concrete poems. Derek owned three of Houédard's
concrete poems, including 'Ciel' and 'News'. One of John Dee's
speeches in Derek's handwritten scripts for *Jubilee* breaks into a
'concrete' layout at one point.[23] Another work from this series has
pan-pipes glued to it, and above them a piece of glass on which
grasses have been etched, which bears the word, 'PANiC'. Unlike
most of the glass in the series, this is not broken. In its serene
simplicity and its classicism this seems almost as if a work by

another prominent concrete poet, Ian Hamilton Finlay.[24] Arguing for a connection with concrete poetry, as I am doing here, also accepts that the words are completely integral to the works, which cannot be expected to make their full array of suggestions of meaning without the legible element. After decades of making paintings without words, Derek turned emphatically to words, which from this point on occur in most of his paintings (with the notable exception of the Dungeness landscape series). There was a good reason for this verbal turn within his painting practice, which cannot be sufficiently explained as a naive attempt on the artist's part to spell out a meaning that he felt was not adequately conveyed by the non-verbal parts of the work.

The coming of AIDS from something rumoured in the period 1981–3 to a recognizable illness by 1986 shook gay culture to its foundations in two major ways. First the mortality rate among young men soared. Becoming HIV+ seemed to lead inevitably to death, and with alarming speed. Derek was soon counting his dead friends. Everyone was coming to terms with safe sexual practices, and the question of whether to have a test for HIV was being addressed. Even aside from the basic fear of the result, early on it was thought better not to know, because of the risk of being sacked from one's job or otherwise ostracized. This brings up the second major fear, which was that sexual freedom, which had seemed secure after the Wolfenden Report and the Parliamentary act of 1967, might again be under threat.[25] The right-wing press, Government inertia over the disease and homophobes in public places, raised the possibility of authorized discrimination, some elements even going so far, Derek believed, as to fantasize 'concentration camps'.[26]

A clause was introduced by Parliament into the Local Government Act – its number varied as the Act was variously amended, but it was generally known as Clause 28. This clause made illegal the 'promotion' of 'homosexuality' in education or local government, and the teaching of 'the acceptability of homo-sexuality as a pretended family relationship'. For Derek and others this posed the question of what was meant, exactly. Would this be interpreted to mean any statement which suggested that being gay was normal or acceptable? Would the new clause be used punitively for purposes of discrimination? What about the up to 15 per cent of the population of gay orientation? What would happen to them if, growing up, they were repeatedly told that only heterosexuality was acceptable? Would generations of people again grow up with the feelings that Derek said overshadowed his adolescence, of being 'probably the wickedest person in the world and probably the only one like this'?[27] As if struggling with the disease was not enough (a disease which could perfectly well attack heterosexuals, but which was stigmatized at the time as a gay plague), social attitudes (at least as relayed through elements of the media and government) panicked and hardened against gay life. Homophobes used the fear of AIDS to pursue their hostile purposes. Derek felt that beneath the 'residual manners' of right-wingers 'a perverted nature red in tooth and nail waits to be unleashed on us'. He also felt that 'the generation that had missed out on the pure joy of the 1960s was busy dismantling everything, as if in revenge', the targets also including the welfare state and the broadening of opportunity that the 1960s had begun.[28] Such social dynamics, albeit in slightly changing form, formed the context for the rest of Derek's life.

He was willing to participate in the fray by speaking out. He went public with the news of his diagnosis in 1987, at a time when people considered silence more prudent, and after that engaged in often heated debate about the best way to approach the entire problem. Part of his counter-attack came in an article in *Art Monthly* for March 1988: 'Every man and woman with the virus is on the run. It would be better in my opinion to see the arts banned along with other forms of education than to deprive children of general infor-mation. Then we would know what the real issue is.'[29] The campaign against Clause 28 was lost, partly because in a crucial vote the House of Lords was packed with 'backwoodsmen' (hereditary peers who rarely attended Parliament) to ensure the Act's passage. However, another piece of legislation soon needed to be campaigned against. This was Clause 25 of the Criminal Justice Bill, which appeared to take discriminating steps against gay life.[30] Derek stayed with the more radical voice fighting the issue, working closely from 1990 with the organization OutRage! rather than allying with the assimilationist society Stonewall, which wanted to take a quieter, less confrontational, approach, and he fell out with people, notably Ian McKellen, over this question. He gained considerable respect from many people, both gay and heterosexual, for his willingness to be an active campaigner while others, such as David Hockney, chose instead to remain silent on the whole issue. The controversy could be gruelling – he didn't appreciate being vilified and pilloried in public – but there was some compensation to be derived from the solidarity with equally committed people. The article in *Art Monthly* stated Derek's agenda: 'Films are already "censored" for an imagined consensus . . . now our job is to broaden [the consensus] so that it contains the whole of life, not just a part of it.'

The next film Derek worked on was of the composer Benjamin Britten's *War Requiem*. Britten had set Wilfred Owen's Great War poetry to music in 1963 for a first performance in the rebuilt Coventry Cathedral and Derek worked on the film during 1988, the seventieth anniversary of the end of that war. In later years Derek stated that he didn't know why he had made the film (he was only ever paid £10 for doing so).[31] It wasn't a film he had written. It was more like a commission, and the terms of it necessitated making no changes whatsoever to Britten's work, which had to be presented entire and continuous. Derek was thus putting images to music and words that were already given. Why did he make it, then? He liked the music, which he had listened to during the long and complicated process of cutting together *The Last of England*. There was respect for an earlier gay artist, Britten. There was a net-profit sharing agreement. In addition to respect for the material, he may have felt the wish to be identified with high culture (a recurrent impulse in his work) particularly after being publicly abused and hearing of the ill-considered speeches about homosexuals being in 'cesspits' made by the Chief Constable of Manchester (James Anderton).[32] The film contains some brilliant visual metaphors and amounts to a sustained achievement in the setting of film to music. It reflects Derek's anger and protest, which also come through strongly in various parts of the book that accompanied it.

While working on *War Requiem*, Derek found himself obliged to defend *The Last of England* from a ridiculous attack by Norman Stone in the *Sunday Times*. Stone was making a bit of a name for himself as a Thatcherite pundit. He confessed not to understand *The Last of England*, but condemned it anyway. His argument veered from repudiation of Derek's pessimistic view of the state of the country to attempts at aesthetic comment (he said that older British films were good because they had a beginning, a middle and an end, and that's what films 'should' have). The hapless Stone proved a bit of a punchbag for Derek, whose reply appeared in the same paper a week later:

> Stone's attack is contradictory because it comes from a supporter of a government that professes freedom in the economic market-place yet seems unable to accommodate freedom of ideas . . . My evidence has tradition and history . . . the decay that permeates *The Last of England* is there for all of us to see; it is in all our daily lives, in our institutions and in our newspapers. [British films for a Hollywood market feed] illusions of stability in an unstable world.[33]

In a notebook a few years earlier, Derek had meditated on the question of slick Hollywood-style product. A book, *Learning to*

Dream, had appeared extolling 'The New British Cinema' with the sort of chamber-of-commerce-style inflation normal for promotions of the alleged British Film Renaissance or British Film Year. According to the author, such cinema had been happening without Derek's involvement. In Derek's notes for a protest speech he muses on the use of the word 'dream' and we find a poem: 'dreaming is our person/ it cannot be bought . . . It is the matrix of creation/ creation is not the 'prerogative' of artists/ but of all workers in the mind.'[34] This is another instance of the theme so close to Derek's heart.

In both these counter-attacks Derek is able to step outside the terms set up by the people whose views he is attacking. At least one resource for his original way of thinking was his interest in the occult tradition of magic. In an interview in *Sounds* magazine he had clarified that influence, specifying its particular value and citing John Dee and Jung as important rather than Aleister Crowley (the self-styled 'Beast' with a reputation for magic). 'I found that things I had been doing unconsciously which might have seemed slightly aimless actually had a centre . . . it distances you from the way most people are looking at things – it gives you an outsider's viewpoint.' He added advice for readers: 'Enjoy yourself as much as you possibly can, because you only live once . . . Go out and dance.'[35] The value specified in this interest in occultism is psychological in a broad sense.

In 1988, undeterred by all the pebbles and the lack of soil, Derek started making his garden in earnest at Prospect Cottage, planting nineteen varieties of rose. The garden has a metaphorical value which is connected with its setting, particularly the nuclear power station not far away. To a casual visitor Dungeness seems strange and un-English, with no trees, hedges, walls or lawns. Given the proximity of the power station, it might seem to such a visitor as if all those conventional features, together with the soil itself, have been blasted or burned away by some sort of nuclear accident. In other words, for a moment it looks like a modern secular version of the Waste Lands of Arthurian myth. In the late 1980s especially, after Three Mile Island in the USA, Chernobyl in the Soviet Union and the open secret of problems at Windscale (Sellafield) in the UK, nuclear accident or catastrophe began to seem inevitable rather than unimaginable. To a visitor expecting danger from the nuclear industry, the landscape looks as if blighted. With no visible soil, and in the presence of what to many seemed a giant brooding threat, Derek's act of gardening seems a defiantly life-affirming struggle against an unfavourable situation, triumphantly carried out.

That struggle has its concrete enactment at a different level. This is the level of garden forms, constituted by small-scale features that combine in a fascinating way man-made and natural elements. Found objects that are themselves part of the setting are pressed into service juxtaposed with plants to make the features of the garden. These found objects are things that most people would see no beauty in, or would see their value exhausted. They bring a connotation of collage, of *art brut* or *arte povera*, of a garden made by an 'Outsider'.[36] They include barnacled rusty iron shoes on the upturned feet of old posts, for example, or a rusty old hoe, used for the sake of their triangular shapes, their satisfying red-brown colour, their age-value and because they too, like many of the plants employed, are local. Triangular tops to the upright features help integrate the garden with the electricity pylons in the distance. Pebbles with holes in, or the bones of crabs, are impaled on drift-wood sticks to provide more of the garden's much-needed uprights in the horizontal spaces of the Ness, but it is the man-made features that provide other memorable forms. Springs; chains arranged into circular forms around posts; bulbous metal buoys and floats; battered oil cans; ten-inch spikes; cork floats; a wheel-brace; the tines of an old fork; a cast-iron spoon; an auger and other indes-cribable metal objects all contributed their density of weight, colour and form. For a while even the giant plaster foot that

Prospect Cottage, a detail of the garden in 2010.

Derek had rescued from the Slade's cast room was taken out into the garden.[37] Derek favoured wood and metal. Such relics of commercial fishing and of wartime defences, collected in the garden, concentrate the cultural message of the surrounding territory, and integrate the garden with its setting. Derek tended not to use the plastic objects that wash up relatively plentifully on the beach, bringing with them another sort of cultural message, but his neighbour Brian Yale employed them to make a plastic garden in direct emulation of Derek's. The juxtapositions of colour and form gained from this activity at Prospect Cottage are well illustrated in Howard Sooley's photographs.[38]

Completing the formal level by supplying the other half of the equation for each of the features, but also being an element that works independently and is perhaps more important, is the plant-life. This is where Howard Sooley became a genuine collaborator on the garden after 1991.[39] Here, as we saw in chapter One, Derek had to improvise and adapt to the environment, as did his plants. Some plants growing locally became favourites in the garden, particularly *Crambe maritima*, sea-kale (together with its ornamental relative *Crambe cordifolia*, giant sea-kale). In his writings Derek describes the different stages of growth that these plants go through during the year, shown in Sooley's photographs: the purple spring shoots, glaucous summer foliage, flowers like cloudlets on long stalks well above the leaves, and their subsequent pale green seeds. Each stage of the plant's life cycle had its own contribution to make to the garden's colours, forms and depths of space. In this era sea-kale was not normally considered a garden plant, so Derek is describing a genuine discovery in that respect. He also noticed that the true parasite, dodder, grows on the Ness and he planted santolina, fennel, lavender, rosemary, irises, sedums, red semper-vivums, rue, wallflowers, and near the back door a fig tree. Horned yellow poppy and blue viper's bugloss came into the garden from

Prospect Cottage's garden (*Crambe maritima*, *Crambe cordifolia*, *Rosa mundi*, elder, iris, horse-radish and other plants by the kitchen window), 2010.

the Ness, as did elder and the dark-green gorse and broom, both brightly yellow-flowered.

The house, painted black with deep yellow trim, stands in the middle of the garden. It is integrated with the garden not only by the views its windows provide but by an extraordinary feature. A shortened version of a poem, 'The Sunne Rising' by the seventeenth-century poet John Donne, is inscribed in black letters on the black-painted exterior south wall of the house. These wooden letters, in elegant script, are fixed to the wall so that the shadows they cast project them three-dimensionally proud of the surrounding black paint and allow the poem to be read:

Busie old foole unruly Sunne
why dost thou thus
through windows and through curtaines call on us?
Must to thy motions loves seasons run?
Sawcy Pedantique wretch goe chide
Late schoole boyes and sowre Prentices
goe tell court-huntsmen that the King will ride
call countrey ants to harvest offices
love all alike no Season knowes nor clyme
Nor houres dayes monthes which are the rags of time
Thou Sunne art halfe as happy as wee
in that the worlds contracted thus
thine age askes ease and since thy duties bee
to warme the world that's done in warming us
Shine here on us and thou art everywhere
this bed thy centre is these walls thy spheare

The poem is entirely appropriate to the situation of the house at Dungeness, which Derek believed to be the sunniest place in Britain. It also describes the sunbeams poking their way inside the house to disturb the lovers whose sanctuary it is: thus the poem integrates Prospect Cottage with its setting conceptually. Inside the cottage other features strengthen the integration of inside and outside: doors to the rooms are fitted with small windows where Derek etched the glass; the bedroom door is etched with a picture of ferns, while the door to the work room bears Derek's poem 'I walk in this garden . . .'.

Making the garden involved feeling his way, particularly with respect to the plants that could survive the peculiar conditions, which might not be well represented in average nurseries and garden centres. In *Modern Nature* Derek describes gardening activities and the plants involved, and the way in 1990 that he had started 'the change to the wild plants that grow in Dungeness: cabbages, valerian, daisy'.[40] By the third page of the book he has mentioned the 25 garden plants and the 15 wild plants of the Ness that formed the basis of his garden. The book is presented as a diary, a literary form that implies all the immediacy of experience being recorded with only rough and ready editing. In addition to being a contribution to the literature of the gardening diary, and therefore able to interest a large audience of garden lovers, the book is a very fine piece of the new nature writing, over fifteen years before *Granta* magazine popularized that phrase. Derek's descriptions of the Ness, its peculiarities, its vegetation, its lights, colours and weathers, the phenomenon of its inhabitants, are striking and memorable, and contribute a new variation to the long tradition of British topographical writing.

One of the book's themes is memory, and it bears out Derek's contention in *Kicking the Pricks* that 'the past is present'.[41] There is an amazing portrait of his father. Despite the spontaneous diary form of the book, the author takes his autobiographical episodes in chronological sequence. There is also a great deal of frank description of sexual activities, leavening the garden diary and the nature writing with a strong additional ingredient seeking to convey the realities of queer life. In one section doubts about his life and works are expressed, which leads him to think about the deaths of friends and the lack of queer autobiography. Thinking about AIDS is juxtaposed to thoughts about his time at Canford School – the association linking these topics is that of misery.[42] But despite the gloom of the disease, not the least value of the book is that, amidst the biographical thoughts, the author's sense of humour comes over clearly. A hot night in the gay club 'Heaven' becomes a sort of hell (p. 83); he describes his own appearance, 'scarlet-eyed, bat's ears, complexion like a shrivelled conker' (p. 233). In the second half of the book there is a plaintive and harrowing account of becoming seriously ill, which he was for much of 1990: 'I do not wish to die . . . yet. I would like to see my garden through several summers' (p. 310).

Despite the fevers, the weight loss, the exhaustion, the itching and rashes, the tuberculosis, the extremity of illness that needed long hospital stays, Derek didn't die in 1990 and, after recovering, in 1991–2 painted a series of beautiful paintings, the Dungeness landscape series. In these works he applied paint in thick bands, working the surface energetically, including scoring it through from a bottom-left to top-right direction with the stump of a broken screwdriver. When the works were exhibited in Folkestone in 2001 the paint in some was still sticky, so thickly had it been applied.[43] The details in these paintings are immensely absorbing, the surfaces succulent and exciting. In their brightness, exuding a shimmering colour, at first sight the works seem wild and abstract. Can Dungeness really be *this* deep blue, this blood red? Yet these paintings date from immediately after two of the years of England's 'great summers'[44] (1989 and 1990) when temperatures soared, water became scarce, trees wilted, everything burned in the sunlight. The atmosphere of burning and shimmering in them can be understood as a response. In any case, there is plenty of colour in this landscape, including bright red sempervivums in Derek's garden and an often deep blue sea. Derek exaggerated colour no more than did Van Gogh that of southern France, and his love of the place comes over strongly from this series. 'The swelling in my heart', he wrote about beginning the first paintings, 'throws itself into the reds and gold, floats in cerulean, drowns in the cobalt and hides in the deep sage-green of sadness.' The following day, at the Royal Academy, he saw 'Braque and Vlaminck my favourite fauves with violet and mauve skies. Back to the drawing table at Prospect.'[45]

The paintings might still seem remarkably abstract, especially if compared with Brian Yale's crisply painted naturalistic depictions of a single feature (the lighthouse, or a yellow aeroplane) or the painter Derek Hedgecock's happy and affecting impressionist canvases of fishing boats and wild flowers at Dungeness. From the series we could select one in particular as an example. Yet if we compare it to a photograph of a broom plant growing close to the garden of Prospect Cottage (dark green broom that has pink

Dungeness Landscape (one of a series by that name), *c*. 1991–2, oil on canvas.

dodder growing on it), it suddenly becomes apparent that the painting is hardly abstracted at all. Instead we can take it as a faithful impression: a surprisingly naturalistic depiction of a small piece of the landscape of Dungeness. As Derek put it, the garden contained 'scarlets and blues . . . fire-bright in the wind'.[46] Several of the paintings appear to show Dungeness at night or in the evening, with the illuminated power station sailing in the background.

The garden of Prospect Cottage partly represents Dungeness, and is in its turn represented by its maker in a variety of media: a book (with two posthumous books to follow) Sooley's photographs, a series of paintings. To these we should add a film, *The Garden* (1990).

In this film Derek imagines the story of Christ as a story of a gay couple. In other words, he uses the myth of Christ to dramatize the martyrdom of his form of sexuality. At the time of *War Requiem* one of his targets had been the Christian Church. He wrote in that film's book, 'in my heart I dedicate my film of *War Requiem* to all those

The parasitic plant dodder growing on broom at Dungeness.

cast out, like myself, from Christendom. To my friends who are dying in a moral climate created by a church with no compassion.'[47] In his next film, *The Garden*, Christianity is considered directly, and one aim in casting Christ as a gay couple is to repossess the moral compassion of Christ's life for gay life. Some memorable shots in *War Requiem*, notably a triumphant use of Piero della Francesca's *Resurrection of Christ*, intimate the beginning of this process. Many of the attacks on Derek personally and on homosexuality in general during the 1980s had been undertaken by intolerant Christianists in the names of Christ and God. *The Garden* takes the story of Christ back from them and gives it to the queer community.

The myth of Christ constitutes a major part of the film, but not all of it; much is dedicated to showing the landscape of Dungeness and the garden that gives the film its title. The film ran into problems of various kinds which left their mark on it. Derek had wanted to make another Super-8 film, but instead the production committed him to using 16 mm, which, being more cumbersome, requires a crew. He grumbled about this energetically in *Modern Nature*: 'Glaring faults everywhere . . . 16 mm deadly, with no resonance.'[48] Some problems also stem from the film's concept. There is too much Christ narrative in the final film and not enough landscape. The landscape sequences, largely shot in Super-8, are compellingly beautiful, and the Christ narrative seems improvised by comparison. I would happily exchange scenes of old men in togas tormenting Christ for more haunting scenes of Dungeness.

Derek was also ill for much of the period of post-production on the film (and for this film, as for all his films, post-production was the most important period, during which the film came together). His concentration inevitably wavered. His own comments for December 1989 in *Modern Nature* hint that his particular brand of film-making (featuring visual and conceptual improvisation) was pushed to its limit in this film.[49] The actress who mimes to the song 'Think Pink' was filmed the day after Derek heard about

The Garden (1990).

her. On the eve of filming he still hadn't cast an actor in the part of Christ, so pressed Keith ('Kevin') Collins and Johnny Mills into service to play Christ as a couple. During filming he realized that he hadn't given them anything to do, so ordered up a bath to put them in. It has to be said that this pair of untrained actors, hastily pushed together, are unable to animate the film with a psychologically convincing portrayal of a loving couple. In their defence it has to be said that it is easier to act if you are given some lines to say or at least something to do. That Derek found himself having to improvise in this respect after shooting had started, shows the clash with the more static demands of 16 mm and thus how this film really pushed his methods of film-making to the limit. With the exception of *Blue*, which was radically experimental in a completely different way, his remaining films were to be scripted and shot in more orthodox fashion.

The finished film, though, has great strengths as well as these weaknesses. The landscape sequences stand out. Collins claims a genuine cinematic 'first' in the use of Blue Screen with Super-8. And, in particular, the film centres creativity in the garden, which becomes the seat of the imagination and its grasp upon the world. It is here that we see Derek, near the end of the film, writing in his notebook and closing it: a notebook which we understand to contain the film that we are watching. The garden is at Dungeness, the scenes of the film are around the garden as far as the Listening Wall at Greatstone; everything is integrated by this space that lies at the centre of the film. The mythic spaces that haunt the film are the gardens of Gethsemane and Eden, but the material garden is where we see Derek working and conceiving the film as well as participating in it by being shown working, so that the imagination of conceiving the film becomes part of the film: this is a meditation on creativity centred in the garden. The garden is a real and practical space of creation: the film tries to remind us of its multi-sensory and experiential character with shots of Derek working, planting, watering, burning in the sunshine.

8

Filming Plays, Painting Words, Being Ill

The year 1990 had been a disastrous one for Derek's health. He was admitted to hospital four times: in March–April for tuberculosis of the liver; in May–June for PCP, a form of pneumonia that is an early sign of AIDS. Toxoplasmosis attacked his eyesight in July–August, and in September he was back in hospital with appendicitis. He survived, but decided to take the controversial drug AZT, though in lower doses than the damaging amounts formerly prescribed to patients. Perhaps as a result of the drug he experienced two years of improved health, although he lacked the full energy of the years before 1990. From this time on, the character of his life shifted, as ill-health either gained ground or, while being kept at bay, remained a constant anxiety, draining time and energy. Disease became increasingly one of his themes, in writing, painting and, ultimately, film.

After *The Garden*, Derek's next film, *Edward II* (1991), brings to the fore the questions involved in filming plays. Derek had once contemplated writing a book on the relationship between film and theatre, but abandoned the idea.[1] He was very well placed to understand the constellation of difficulties that such an undertaking leads a film-maker into. His training in Theatre Design at the Slade left him with a thorough understanding of how the symbolism of the theatre emerges through design strategies, and this understanding had been enhanced and augmented by the fourteen theatrical productions he had worked on in various capacities since that time (including opera and ballet). In 1978–9 he had made a film of Shakespeare's play *The Tempest* (1612). He now turned his hand to Christopher Marlowe's play *Edward II* (1592).

Before we turn to that film it would be wise to sketch in some outlines of the problems inherent in filming plays. The practice is beset by complicated questions, and in the present format an extensive discussion is not possible, but three propositions can be advanced that bear upon the issue. The first is that live performances of plays do not depend for their success on realism or naturalism. Madame de Staël understood this point in 1810:

> though we consent to believe that the actors, separated from us by a few planks, are Greek heroes who died three thousand years ago, it is certain that what we call the illusion doesn't consist in believing that what one sees really exists: a tragedy can only appear true to us by the emotion that it causes in us.[2]

Thus although it takes place in the audience's real time using real people as actors within a space that is connected to the audience's real space, a theatrical production of a play is not inherently realist in its mode of representation. The play depends upon the emotion it generates, and its production works in an inherently symbolic mode. An extraordinarily influential book from Derek's first year of professional activity, Peter Brook's *The Empty Space* (1968) reiterates these ideas, and discusses theatre's symbolic modes and their relationship with illusionary realism. So inherently symbolic is theatre that any element of realism has to be carefully and laboriously striven for by stage managers, set designers and producers.

The second proposition is one about film. A conventional feature film, in contrast to plays in the theatre, embodies a thirst for realism or naturalism. We might think that this is because film is based in photography, but in greater part the realism of film is a conventional mode of representation that entire crews of technicians strive to induce. It is wholly conventional yet entirely built into the system of orthodox feature film production. Every few years a new invention (improved sound, digital special effects) is employed to enhance the realism of the film.

Third proposition: the result of feature film's thirst for realism is that when called upon to film a play it tends to destroy the play that it is attempting to film. By definition a play can only live through its symbolism and emotion. The realist mode of film, heavily financially capitalized, overwhelms the symbolism of the play. David Hare's *Plenty* (1978, filmed in 1985) or Alan Bennett's *The History Boys* (2004, filmed 2006) are good examples of truly outstanding plays that made mediocre films, not through any shortage of talent among the film-makers (in the latter case the writer, director and cast were the same as in the theatre) but simply through being conceived utterly conventionally within the feature film mode. As a play *The History Boys* was excellent; as a film, ordinary, simply because it didn't attempt to preserve enough theatrical qualities in the new medium. The best parts of the film are when the boys act: that is, when they act out in the classroom without other props, costumes or settings the endings of the films *Now Voyager* and *Brief Encounter*, and those moments are purely theatrical values in which we see completely different human dilemmas being successfully dramatized.

Derek recognized the danger of naturalistic film destroying symbolic theatre at the time of making his third feature film, *The Tempest*, when there was no model available to him other than that of the orthodox studio-based feature film. 'For *The Tempest* we needed an island of the mind that opened mysteriously like Chinese boxes, an abstract landscape so that the delicate description in the poetry, full of sound and sweet airs would not be destroyed by Martini lagoons . . . I sailed as far away from tropical realism as possible.'[3] In programme notes for a screening of *The Tempest* at the London Film Festival in 1979 Derek made the point in more general terms: 'I have always felt that Shakespeare translates rather badly into film. There is a great rift between the artificiality of stage conventions and the naturalism of film settings.'

The question recurred twelve years later for *Edward II*: how do you film a play without destroying it? While conditions of production ambition had changed (Channel Four's funding of films made for television had begun, and BBC Films, which financed *Edward II*, was willing to extend its productions to feature films) there were still few models for the task of filming a play for television and cinema. As in the former case, of course, Derek was not taking a specific production out of the theatre and putting it into a film. Rather he was turning the written play into a film, while attempting to do justice to the fact that it was a play by retaining some of the aesthetics, values and experience of a play.

One of the ways to retain these qualities involved trusting his actors to act, rather than the film-maker mincing up their performances into fragments with the predictable frequent cuts and restless editing techniques of normal feature film. For example, the joyful reunion of Edward and Gaveston upon the latter's return from exile is filmed in the middle distance, shot through one static camera and a continuous take. A string quartet plays while the king waits; a tense Edward signals to them to change the tune; Gaveston appears and the pair perform a silly joyful dance before stumbling around laughing.

Another way of retaining some flavour of theatrical values involved staging. How do you stage exile? A conventional feature film might take a crew to Calais, hunt for a suitably medieval street corner, rent it for half a day, and film Gaveston lounging discontentedly on it; alternatively such a setting could be lovingly recreated on set by carpenters and set decorators. Instead Derek put his actor on a bare stage rock against a black background of night and deluged rainwater over him while he howled like an unhappy animal. In both this and the reunion scene, historical fidelity and period local colour and detail are sacrificed for a more ambitious goal. Both of these scenes work well because they are dedicated to conveying the feelings inherent in the human dilemmas – precisely what Madame de Staël identified as the dramatic element.

How else do you film a play? In Derek's case, you trust that other types of symbolic staging specific to theatre will come through in the final film in a satisfactory way. One scene shows, in one take through a single camera, Isabella and Mortimer walking in conversation from one (left) side of the set to an exit at the right rear, at a pace sufficient for them to say their lines in the time available. In another shot a huntsman guides hounds across the set behind the action. We understand that they are inside a studio set, yet they bring with them the symbolic values of both the circus (where animals are marshalled in theatrical performance) and the outdoors. These two examples are about retention of the movement and presence of theatrical performance. You also avoid, as much as possible, the poor old threadbare grammar of film (shot/reverse shot: eyeline shot, etc.). In an undated typescript entitled 'EXHAUSTION' Derek wrote 'God I hate the feature film, its so expected, the story that's been told to death, the photography that's perfect yet again, the acting tuned to the dullness of perfection'.[4] Here he is exclaiming against the formulaic character of feature film. Instead, in *Edward II* he trusted the devices of theatre to be able to register an impact even in film. Peter Brook discusses Brechtian alienation devices as invitations to the audience to exercise judgement. Such devices, disturbing the smooth unfolding of the plot through some uncanny interruption, are recurrent features of theatrical performances, and not confined to Brecht (although taken to one of their extreme points in his work): 'each rupture is a subtle provocation and a call to thought'.[5]

Surely in such devices we have an explanation of a recurrent feature of Derek's films, but one which film critics at the time universally failed to understand in such a way: the use of anachronism. When the seventeenth-century banker in *Caravaggio* holds a pocket calculator, Derek is not trying to be funny, but to get us to think about parallels between past and present – his interest is the interpretation of the past. What's at stake in the many anachronisms of *Edward II*, a film which Derek in part at least saw as a contribution to current battles over queer rights and difficulties, is less a question about the interpretation of the past than an enlisting of King Edward, Marlowe and his play in the contemporary struggle. In other words, the anachronisms invite the audience to reflect on the current predicament of queer life via this comparison with the queer renaissance playwright's treatment of the queer medieval king. Alienation devices prevent the audience watching in a 'state of anaesthetized uncritical belief'[6] – precisely the state that the conventional feature-film industry deploys huge material resources to induce.

Derek constantly grumbled about small budgets for his films, yet something was probably created by imposed economy. If in conventional feature films the budget is large enough to reduce any problem in staging to the realist/naturalistic mode, a predictable way of working can destroy symbolic values. Brook discusses 'Rough Theatre', which, deprived of huge financial means, improvises: 'a bucket will be banged for a battle, flour used to show faces white with fear'.[7] In other words, constrained budgets enforce improvisation, bring out creativity and so contribute to more symbolic solutions. The effects of magic in Derek's *The Tempest* worked this way; at least one was purely nineteenth century in technology, when Ariel is suddenly brightly lit off-camera to be reflected from an (itself unseen) mirror in a darkened corner of the location so that he seems to hang in the air above Prospero's head. In *Edward II* it is perhaps the staging of the civil war that shows most economy

Rough theatre: *Edward II* (1991).

of means: a map, a naked light bulb, duffel coats and battledress conjure it up, rather than large numbers of extras running around in exploding countryside. The symbolically complicated final scene, in which the dishevelled Mortimer and Isabella are locked in a cage, their faces whitened, while the child Edward III, arrayed in lipstick and earrings, dances triumphantly on top of the cage to 'The Dance of the Sugar Plum Fairy', also qualifies as a piece of Rough Theatre.

Edward II also manifests an extreme economy by means of its symbolic references. In a prime example, a heightened violence is suggested by the ox carcass in which the soldier/policeman who murdered Gaveston is hung up to be cruelly killed by Edward and Spencer. This carcass is simultaneously a homage both to Rembrandt's painting *Flayed Ox* (1655) and to the work of Francis Bacon, who used Rembrandt's image repeatedly, including in *Painting* (1946).

An objection can be made that Derek failed to raise the actors' levels in saying the words; to put it another way, the words were not made to work hard enough, which was the actors' task.[8] Given that the play was written by the inventor of the eloquence and range of blank verse, 'Marlowe's mighty line', this is a serious critical point. A similar objection was also made about the film of *The Tempest* by the scholar Frank Kermode.[9] Nevertheless, this caveat apart, *Edward II* sets the international standard for how to film a play. It won awards at film festivals in Venice and Amsterdam and was almost universally critically acclaimed.

Shooting for *Edward II* took place in February–March 1991, and the film was screened in the Edinburgh and Venice festivals by the end of the summer that year, opening later in London and in March 1992 in the USA. Throughout 1991 Derek was busy. He supported the newly formed campaigning group, Outrage, attending demonstrations and gay parades (designed among other things to lower the age of consent between consenting males to 16, and to demand social acceptance). This involvement with Outrage helped to shape both *Edward II* and the book published to accompany the film, *Queer Edward II*. Early in 1991 Derek met Howard Sooley, who became a collaborator in the garden at Prospect Cottage, where Derek also started to keep bees. *Modern Nature* was published, favourably reviewed in some broadsheets and condemned in others. Derek worked on scripts for projects ultimately left unrealized ('Bliss', 'Pansy'). Between October and Christmas he wrote a personal view of gay life from the 1940s to the present moment, inevitably partial but also very engaging: *At Your Own Risk: A Saint's Testament*. His writing is entirely effective, and the book is suffused with strong feelings about the injustice with which human beings have treated each other.

Activism around queer life featured friendships with a group of like-minded public intellectuals like Peter Tatchell, Alan Beck, Nicholas de Jongh, Simon Watney and Sarah Graham, with a corresponding high level of mental stimulus. The demonstrations, parades and life as a public personality continued.

In 1989 Derek had staged an installation on the theme of queer life at the Third Eye Centre in Glasgow. It had featured objects covered with tar and feathers, printed ephemera including gay erotica and newspaper homophobia, and as its centrepiece two men in bed together behind a curtain of barbed wire. Manchester City Art Gallery now invited him to mount a solo art exhibition in May–June 1992. He borrowed a studio and an assistant from Richard Salmon and made a series of large, colourful paintings: the *Queer* series. One of them was bought by the Arts Council, and to exemplify the series *Morphine* is a good example (at present exhibited in the library of the Arts University College, Bournemouth). It consists of oil paint thickly applied to a surface formed by multiple copies of an issue of one of the gutter newspapers that had been printed with a homophobic report on the front page. A young actor was being crucified in the press for his sexual orientation. Derek's response was to plaster the surface with thickly applied paint (this might in part have been necessary to get the paint to adhere to a slick surface) and score through the paint in a random pattern of marks: activity is particularly intense around the left middle of the work. The work effectively blots out the press report except for the headline, 'Storm over East Ender Rent boy FILTH get this garbage off TV'. The headline and newspaper have been abused in their turn by Derek in black and red paint sometimes applied quite dry, yet thick, spread and scored by a variety of instruments. A scored word, MORPHIN, stretches right across the work, above a second word MORPHINE painted by finger in yellow paint over wet black, which is itself applied over a thinner layer of red. The yellow paint barely sticks and the finger's pressure has wiped off all layers of paint except for a thin smear that shows the texture of the canvas backing. Elsewhere thick globules of paint protrude from the surface, apparently angrily and hastily applied. The newspaper's hypocrisy is only made plainer by the words 'Red Nose Special' (a charity appeal) next to the paper's banner.

'Morphin' is slang for shape-changing, while morphine obliterates pain. Derek's paint has obliterated the specifics of the

Morphine, 1992, oil on canvas, 251.5 × 179 cm.

newspaper's hate. Of course, the situation is not as simple as this. We can still see what has happened in general terms: homophobia is still in circulation. At the bottom of the work – as far as possible from the headline – Derek allows to appear a small portrait photograph of the young man martyred by this particular report, as if out of respect for his humanity and fellow-feeling for his predicament. In works such as this, Derek's aesthetics became an ethics.

In the ethics was a huge anger. In July he made a work, *40% of British Women*, using a newspaper's report about a woman who accused a young man of giving her AIDS through unprotected sex that had involved buggery. The newspaper seemed to be particularly inflamed since this was a heterosexual incident, as if AIDS should be confined to a manageable ghetto of queer life where it could be ignored. A subheadline reads, 'He called it love . . . But I call it murder.' Derek wrote in yellow/orange paint over the copies of the story:

SODOMY STRAIGHT

HERE'S NEWS FOR YOU

40% OF BRITISH WOMEN

TAKE IT UP THE ARSE

YOU CALLED IT MURDER

BUT I CALLED IT LOVE

SPREAD THE PLAGUE

Murder is, of course, a crime, punishable by life in prison. Much hinges, no doubt, on whether the carrier of HIV knew that he was infected or not but, leaving that issue aside, various questions come to mind. Should love-making be classified as a crime? Should people be sent to prison for acts of love-making, or pilloried for them in the gutter press? Derek wrote in his diary, 'The witch hunts of the tabloids and in this case dotty Labour MPS – Clare Short said his name should be published, what about confidentiality? Hardly words of wisdom or comfort.'[10] If people were to be sent to prison as carriers of HIV, why not for syphilis? Is the determining factor the state of medical science with respect to the two diseases? The era when homosexuality was considered both a disease and a custodial offence loomed up like a ghost from the past. The furious words emblazoned across the work are totally uncompromising and the last line is styled to seem irresponsible. Was Derek, stricken by AIDS, really urging that the plague should be spread in hetero-sexual society by buggery of women? Contemplating some reviews of the *Queer* exhibition, Derek wrote in January 1993, 'one day the paintings will be seen as more than tantrums and will be seen to be wet with my tears'.[11]

Soon after this incident Derek went to the Tate Gallery and saw Richard Hamilton's 'hospital installation' – 'a hospital bed with a TV on which Mrs T. gives a Party Political Broadcast'.[12] In another painting in the *Queer* series, *Spread the Plague,* a mass of words seems to be constituted within the paint. Many are illegible or obliterated – from some only a letter or two emerges – but the following words can be made out: 'Sweet Queer 16 Soho teenage AIDS vice boys Revenge Blood spread the even plague'. ('Even' is just about the only visible part of the original tabloid newspaper report.) So the AIDS crisis flames up in a welter of hostile and controversial words and arguments rather than being approached rationally by the mass media. That the exhibition was in Manchester must have been particularly satisfying for Derek, as that city's chief constable had become notorious for anti-gay speech.

From early in 1992 Derek was tormented by a parasitic mollus-cum on his face that had to be burned off at regular intervals with liquid nitrogen. His health continued to be delicate, but relatively stable until the virus as CMV attacked his eyesight in August, leading to several disorienting and anxious weeks and loss of vision in his right eye before things stabilized to leave him with a reduced visual field, a strange blank on the right where previously there had been vision. Nevertheless, he managed to hold up well enough to continue working. Three diary entries from 1992 give something of the feeling of Derek's life on the eve of his final period: 'The awful devastation of AIDS has left everyone disillusioned and with little fight' (5 June); 'I sat by the front door [of Prospect Cottage] wafted by the clove-scented pinks, it is an idyll: *et in Arcadia ego*. I am so in love with this place please God I see another year' (6 June); 'The sun set behind the tower of Lydd church in a blaze of pink and purple, and the clouds turned to indigo in a full moon which sailed through them into the night' (12 June).[13] Demonstrated by these entries are the social–cultural crisis, very pessimistic worries about his own health and a continuing relish for the gorgeous spectacles nature provides.

A project for making the film *Wittgenstein* came to Derek as a commission in 1992. Tariq Ali's Bandung company wanted to make a series of films about philosophers for Channel Four. A script for one on Ludwig Wittgenstein (1889–1951) had been obtained from Terry Eagleton, who was a literary critic, neither a practised nor professional scriptwriter. This script was a piece of social realism in the Trevor Griffiths mould.[14] As we have seen from *Kicking the Pricks*, Derek abominated social realism as an aesthetics. He pulled apart the script, and his collaborator and long-term friend Ken Butler, associate director of *Edward II* (he had taken over on the days when Derek had been too ill to attend the filming) turned to Wittgenstein's biography by Ray Monk and put a lot of material derived from it into the new script.[15] So the Wittgenstein who in Eagleton's version tends to strike rather hollow attitudes is replaced by a sort of holy fool of philosophy, played a lot of the time by his childhood self (his biographer had written that the philosopher required 'childlike innocence' in a disciple and at 40 was himself 'still an adolescent'[16]). The difference between the scripts led to bad-tempered rows between Eagleton and Derek, in person and in the press. Here was a cycling round of the dilemma in the film industry with regard to scripts that we saw occupying Derek in the early 1980s. Between first version of the script and final film, what is the property?

The budget was small, really too small for an 80-minute film, and, as Derek said of his film-making in general, 'the budget was the aesthetic'.[17] In the case of *Wittgenstein* the budget paid for two October weeks in a small studio in central London. Interested in Wittgenstein's thoughts on colour, and at the time inspired by them to put together a book of his own thoughts on colour (*Chroma*), Derek decided to paint the studio black and to use bright solid colours for other characters' costumes and for props throughout the film. The exception is the protagonist himself, who is dressed naturalistically in line with a famous photograph of him wearing a tweed jacket and open-necked flannel shirt. As Derek wrote in *Chroma*, black gives an effect of infinity on film, a sense of being 'boundless'.[18] Against this background of infinite space, the brightly lit colours shine out. As a constant contrast with Wittgenstein's costume, those of the other actors amount to a perpetual alienation device, but there were reasons for this emphatic use of colour deriving from Wittgenstein's philosophy. At one point in the film John Maynard Keynes is shown doing a circular jigsaw puzzle, all the pieces of which are white. This is a Jarman/Butler joke inspired by the fact that in *Remarks on Colour* Wittgenstein uses the example of a jigsaw puzzle to illustrate the relative values of colour: the fact that a colour's values are determined by the context in which it appears.[19] In his writings Wittgenstein was much exercised by the logical structure of colour, and the crudeness and subjectivity of our vocabulary for colours; yet in an excellently quirky moment he could write 'colours spur us to philosophize'.[20]

By filming entirely inside a small black studio, by avoiding exterior shots and locations, and through needing to make six minutes of finished film for each day's work (twice the normal amount) Derek essentially turned the project into the film of a play, and indeed into an example of what Peter Brook calls 'The Holy Theatre' which allows the invisible to become sensed and is made possible by a combination of 'small means, intense work, rigorous discipline and absolute precision'.[21] A lot of the sheer expertise contributing to these latter three categories came from Derek's group of friends who wanted to work on this project for very little financial reward because it looked, so precarious was his health, as if it might be his last. Ably supported by Tilda Swinton, Michael Gough, John Quentin, Lynn Seymour, Clancy Chassay as the young Wittgenstein, and indeed the entire cast, Karl Johnson produced a brilliant performance as the awkward philosopher.

As part of his idea that artists must reinvent themselves as artists and spread the creativity around, first voiced in *Jubilee*, Derek had worked on his films since the late 1970s with a shifting group of people whose presence tended to contribute to a friendly positive atmosphere on set. He said that the purpose of film-making was to create community.[22] Now, while he worried about exploiting them because the money was so pitiful, the members of that community were freely paying him back. He had over the years, rather like an early twentieth-century literary editor such as Ford Madox Ford, made 'discoveries': that is, he had recognized talent early, nurtured it with advice and encouraged it with opportunities. This is one of the ways in which Derek's reinvented aesthetics constituted an ethics. Among these discoveries, Toyah Willcox is one example.[23] His greatest successes in this regard must surely be Tilda Swinton, to whom he gave her first step into film, and the costume designer Sandy Powell, whom he advised and nurtured from a time before her first job in film.[24] Both of them wanted to work on *Wittgenstein*, in which Swinton even made her own small but telling design contribution one day, persuading the make-up artists to paint her face in yellow and blue stripes and turning up on the set to surprise Derek with it. He liked it, and it went into the film, a little example of spreading the creativity around.[25] When

Swinton's character confronts Wittgenstein with this face it is she who starts with surprise – which simultaneously suggests the way in which Wittgenstein was felt to be abnormal by his acquaintances, and the probability that he felt them to be outlandish and illogical. The moment also suggests the way in which the film consistently represents things from Wittgenstein's point of view.

Barely a single scene in the film relies on a naturalistic approach (exceptions can be made for the 'rowing to Norway' (scene 11) and those of the battlefields (scenes 15 and 16) – and these exceptions owe much more to theatrical naturalism than filmic). From the moment the young Wittgenstein introduces his family and they appear wearing ancient imperial Roman dress amid crowd sounds, much energy is devoted to defamiliarization, denaturing and alienation devices. At one point a small green Martian character shows the film's code by saying that he knows that 'this film studio is in Waterloo but how do I know that you are Ludwig Wittgenstein?' This is a classic alienation device of 'making strange', inducing the audience to think along Brechtian lines about the film itself. There is some shot/reverse shot in dialogues, but offsetting this employment of realist convention the use of colours, if nothing else, works to denaturalize the action. The film also allows a cinema of small gestures when a sigh or a look from Wittgenstein complete a scene.

The dramatization of Wittgenstein's constrained sexuality happens through a brilliant metaphor. Wittgenstein sits closed within a giant bird-cage. Trapped with him is a parrot in its own smaller cage. Why is this? It provides a symbol for the fact that, while Wittgenstein wished to call into question the fundamentals of things – the foundations of mathematics, of logic, and of philosophy – and thereby to allow philosophy to help people live their lives, he was utterly unable to call into question the fundamentals of his own nature, and to accept it despite society's ban, so being able to go forward happy with his homosexuality.

Wittgenstein (1992).

In this crucial area of life he was subject to determinism – unable to exercise free will. He says, 'Living in a world where such a love is illegal and trying to live openly and honestly is a complete contradiction. I have known Johnny three times. And each time I began with a feeling that there was nothing wrong. But after, I felt shame.'

The making of *Wittgenstein* had entailed long days of work (7 a.m. until midnight), intense concentration, explanations of concepts to others, cajoling of performances from the actors, a myriad of decisions. Whether in reaction to all this effort or not, in November 1992 Derek suffered a relapse in the form of another attack from PCP, the bacterial pneumonia of 1990. He spent the best part of a month in St Bartholomew's Hospital ('Bart's') in London, losing weight and strength rapidly. When he emerged, the ordeal had taken its toll not only on his health but his appearance. During 1993 the virus provoked constant fevers and attacked Derek's stomach, his skin and his eyesight. At times he was only able to see in shades of grey. His physical strength waned amid stomach upsets, sleepless nights, fevers, muscles wasting, loss of balance and barely a day on which he felt properly healthy. He staggered to the seventh anniversary of his diagnosis at Christmas 1993. By the time he reached it he was blind and in a wheelchair.

During the previous winter (1992–3), however, there had been times when he was working on the post-production of *Wittgenstein*, the book *Chroma* (which a friend nicknamed 'Gingerbits' was typing for him, in Derek's view dawdling over his task) and the film *Blue* simultaneously, sometimes from his hospital bed. *Chroma* is an idiosyncratic and thought-provoking book on colour, incorporating elements of the chemical and cultural histories of colours, but mainly exploring their feeling with great immediacy and vibrancy. Here Derek deploys the full resources of his writing in an attempt to convey a difficult and elusive aspect of a subject in which he had developed a lifetime's expertise. He joined an illustrious line of descent, partly inspired by Wittgenstein, who had himself been reading Goethe on the subject.

One of Derek's main activities in 1993 continued the exploration of colour in another way. The titles of the *Queer* series of paintings (*Blood*, EIIR, *Time*, *Spread the Plague*, *Dead Angels*, *Letter to Minister*, *Queen and Capital*, *Negative Images*, *Act Up*, *Aids Isle* and so on) connote no particular subjectivity. They have a cultural significance, as if the subject-matter lies in the cultural response to the virus. For his next series of paintings Derek changed the emphasis radically.

In 1993 he made the series which was exhibited posthumously (again in Manchester, this time at the Whitworth Art Gallery) as *Evil Queen – The Last Paintings*. This series was not a cultural attack. The gutter press ceased to be of interest to the artist. Two assistants prepared the seven-foot-square canvases and painted them with an initial background colour.[26] Then Derek (and his assistants)[27] would apply paint, in varying patterns and thick-nesses, sometimes flinging it at the canvas, and using hands a great deal. A matrix of smeared and splattered paint sometimes assumes forms, sometimes remains formless as a sequence of handmarks dragged down the canvas. With the exception of the tightly controlled *Germs* and *Infection*, the paintings that are dated from May and June are very thickly impasted with paint to give an extraordinarily visceral effect, while in those dated from the month of October there is much less paint, the handprints and fingermarks have more space between them, and a waning of physical powers is clearly connoted.

Within this series, *Scream* and *Death* give us tunnels to hell. There is a bleak midwinter feeling about *Ouch (Arse Bandit)*, in which the additional words 'shit stabber' are discernible in mauve paint. The extraordinary *Fuck Me Blind* emblazons its words scratched into the surface of a thick band of charcoal-grey paint that extends from one side to the other of the eau-de-nil background. The dark grey paint swirls there like smoke from an industrial chimney, or a cloud. A small amount of angry scarlet paint on the letters F, M and B relieves the atmosphere slightly, but also reminds the viewer of the human blood that is ultimately at issue.

The words discernible in the paintings constitute an integral part of each work. They cannot be said to be afterthoughts. The words of *Arse Injected Death Syndrome* establish a queer atmosphere – using that word to designate gay men's awareness that they live in hostile circumstances, where homoerotic acts and lives are circumstanced with prejudice, and thus adopting the self-designation of 'queer' because it betokens that prejudice and the way in which self-definition is affected by extrinsic definitions. The phrase of the painting, adapted from the initials spelling AIDS, is picked up from a hostile use in street slang and therefore signifies a cultural appropriation. The main point to make about the words in the *Evil Queen* series, however, is that they are more personal and subjective than those of the *Queer* series. In nearly

Ataxia Aids is Fun, 1993, oil on canvas, 251 × 179 cm.

all the paintings the words are applicable to Derek's subjectivity. They can be seen as descriptions of himself. This is what he is: this is what he is allowed to be: he is limited – not only by the disease but by how people view the disease (and therefore him). *Fuck Me Blind* is a hyperbolic slang phrase for pleasure. Yet in a completely literal sense someone in effect had done that to Derek, since he caught the virus during an act of love-making and blindness from toxoplasmosis was one of its symptoms. (During the making of these works his sight had recovered enough to be viable in one eye with huge-lensed glasses.) Another painting's title is *Dizzy Bitch,* a piece of insulting slang condemning a scatter-brained or out-of-control person, but in Derek's ironic employment of it the phrase refers to a feeling of vertigo that the virus brought. The painting donated to the Tate Gallery, *Ataxia Aids is Fun*, has a strong irony attached to its designation of the loss of balance that he was experiencing (he refers to himself in his diary for this period as 'Old Wobble' or 'Mr Legless'[28]). *Scream* is what having the virus makes Derek want to do, while *Death* is where it leads. He finds himself *Impotent*. Things have turned *Topsy Turvy* for this *Evil Queen* (the latter is a straightforward queer statement – how Derek was regarded by sections of the Press and homophobic individuals). He is *Dead Sexy*: having once prided himself on his sexiness, his physical appeal, does he face death as a result? (He would have hated this question to be answered in the affirmative.) Having the virus drives him *Do Lalley*, a slang term deriving from a place in India (Deolali) where a camp was set up for old British soldiers awaiting their return home after having been paid off. Some of them were kept waiting for so long before their ship arrived that they went mad, crazed, do-lally. Eventually, probably soon (from the perspective of June 1993) Derek will *Drop Dead*. (This is of course another pun, this time on 'drop dead gorgeous', an expression of admiration for a person's looks.) There is a bitter irony in the way in which phrases associated with physical attraction and sexual pleasure are transmuted into phrases evoking death and terminal disease.

Of the messes of paint and the intense physicality of its application, Derek spoke of allowing the paintings to 'release the violence in me': the 'anger which everyone with HIV feels'.[29]

The last five in the series, dated October 1993, no longer have the amazing visceral depths of paint and colour characteristic of the paintings from May and June. Here the backgrounds are clearly seen: *Dipsy Do (Sinister)*'s is jade, *Do Lalley*'s mauve; and marks have been made on top of them. All feature handmarks in red paint, as if a prisoner with bleeding fingers has attempted to claw his way through a wall. Andrew Logan says that the handmarks suggest to him a desperate attempt to hang onto life.[30] Yet it is surely equally arguable that they suggest attempts to escape into art. To escape from what? Life? Or death? The interpretations are reconcilable if we accept Logan's view of Derek that 'He was his art.' For the artist an earlier idea of escape lay through the image ('Through the Billboard Promised Land' is a recurring phrase in *A Finger in the Fishes Mouth* designating also escape to America and Pop Art) into the cool calm landscapes of the late 1960s such as *Cool Waters*. So one thing these seemingly desperate handmarks dragged down the canvas suggest is that there is now no escape. At the same time the sparer application of paint, no longer applied in frenzied whirls of smeared, stroked and splattered colours, depths and mixtures, connotes a privation of strength and a waning of physical powers, reflecting Derek's predicament as 1993 went on. The idea of progressive weakening becomes part of the art.

Conventional art-historical approaches might suggest two things about these series of paintings. The method adopted in the *Queer* series could be seen as akin to Jasper Johns' use of pieces of newspaper dipped in encaustic and adhering to cloth to constitute his *Flag*, an early piece of Pop Art. There too the newspaper fragments can be read through the surface and so function on the level of content of the work. Robert Rauschenberg's works, in which he reproduced found images by silk-screening for incorporation in his paintings also come to mind, perhaps more appropriately. The other might be seek to define the *Evil Queen* series as Expressionist.[31] In the 1960s Derek had very firmly rejected both Pop Art and Abstract Expressionism in favour of his figurational, non-gestural, non-Expressionist landscape paintings which were cool, dispassionate, mathematical, belonging, if to any line of descent, to one including Paul Nash's *Equivalents for the Megaliths* and the work of artists such as Julian Trevelyan. It was as if Derek waited to employ the techniques of Pop Art and the Abstract Expressionists until there was a very good personal reason for doing so.

Part of Derek's rejection of Pop in the 1960s was no doubt because Pop didn't allow artists complete freedom of choice. Their subject-matter existed in the culture, came from outside, was a given, and the question became how to deal with it. In the decisions surrounding that question existed the (only) room for creative manoeuvre. However, by 1993, as HIV gave way to AIDS, Derek's circumstances had changed irrevocably: circumstances from outside impinged upon him emphatically and his response amounted to the only free will he had left. He had not espoused Pop or Abstract Expressionism simply as trends in art in the 1960s, but now his situation demanded the resources of those movements if it was to be met head-on. It seems that Derek did not want to choose, or try to choose, a promised land through the billboard, but to face his circumstances squarely.

In making this series of extremely honest self-exposures, from a position of extreme physical debilitation (just a few months before he died) Derek achieved an ethics within his painting aesthetics. Exposing the effect the virus has on his body and his sense of himself, he testifies to an aspect of the suffering it was causing

Ataxia Aids is Fun (detail).

to many others as well as him, but he does so with great clarity and exemplary artistic control. The 'master-spell' of irony in his words guards against self-pity while not inhibiting the expression of feelings of fury, bitterness and outrage. His artistic poise is not in question, however much his physical powers might have been declining.

In the *Evil Queen* series the painted matrix within or out of which the words appear is not separable or disposable. The word 'Scream', painted across a canvas on its own, would not have the power that Derek's *Scream* achieves with its moulded masses of bilious pus-yellow and pink paint. We gaze into a horrible tunnel. The word is indelibly associated with Edvard Munch's masterpiece of Expressionist art, and serves by its homage to establish Derek's series as Expressionist.

The effect of the early-summer 1993 paintings, with their poured and splattered paint sometimes apparently flung at the canvas, is visceral and physical. Just as physical, though in a less threatening way (presenting themselves more as a spectacle) are the crazed scrapings and scratchings of paint by seemingly hyperactive though enfeebled hands in the works from October. I would like to argue that the integration of word and paint in these works relate them to the extensions of the concrete poetry Derek had achieved in some of his black series of the mid 1980s. The *Evil Queen* series is a further extension, well beyond the point reached in the earlier series and represents a change in the way Derek employed words. In the earlier works the words were etched on glass and applied by adhesion to the paint surface, so they have a handwritten form, a calculated spatial distribution and a size related to handwriting. In their whiteness they also contrast with the matrix of black paint. In the *Evil Queen* series the words have obviously taken on a wild and vigorous life of their own, invading and occupying the paint surface, dwelling within it, shaping its forms. The words in *Infection*, *Fuck Me Blind* and *Scream* are scored deeply into the paint. *Ouch (Arse Bandit)* is constituted differently, the words so thoroughly worked into the surface of the paint that their letters largely form the work, as is the case with *Death*. The black paint of the words *Bubble & Squeak* is essential to the completion of this painting made of scarlet marks on a yellow background. *Topsy Turvy*, as befits its title, is an exception, there being no words within its firework-like surface. In the case of the Tate Gallery's *Ataxia Aids is Fun* the words emerge from the complicated layers of paint. Indeed, two further phrases in addition to the work's title emerge from the paint as the viewer gazes at it. These phrases are not immediately perceptible and take time to manifest themselves. The word ATAXIA occurs with an emphatic horizontal emphasis in paint underpinning its triangular jagged forms. A detail shows that the word has been envisaged, and prepared for, very early on in the painting process. The words are also fundamental to the overall colour scheme, as mauve is only employed around the letters, occurring nowhere else. As in this case, so in the whole series: none of the verbal element is an afterthought.

Words have a crucial importance in Derek's other last undertaking, also from 1993 – his final work in film, *Blue*.

9

In the End, the Poet

After August 1992 Derek divided his time between the Phoenix
House flat, Prospect Cottage and hospital beds, with time at
Dungeness being increasingly squeezed by mounting ill-health.
Tormented by locomotor ataxia, by boils in his rectum, in March
and April 1993 Derek was in Bart's Hospital again, attacked by a
fever and an extremely painful burning and itching skin condition,
suspected of having contracted another virus, MAI. ('My face', he
wrote in his diary, 'like a purple baboon's arse in a snowstorm'.[1])
He developed an intermittent but persistent upset stomach,
becoming subject to attacks of diarrhoea in public places and
at night in bed. This persisted for the remainder of his life. The
illnesses contributed greatly to destroying his strength but didn't
altogether erode his will to continue the struggle. He lost weight
and his appearance changed to that of a frail thin aged man. He
managed to spend periods at Dungeness and gained strength
from looking after the garden there. More than anything else,
though, the relationship with Collins kept him going. The last
published diary, *Smiling in Slow Motion* (2000) represents its
author to be in good spirits, at least much of the time, until the
end of the summer of 1993, particularly relishing a holiday in
France with his friend the gardener and photographer Howard
Sooley. They visited Monet's garden at Giverny and found Jean
Cocteau's chapel at Millet le Forêt. From September the diary
starts to tail off. If we take an interest in writing about himself

to be an index of his will to live and enjoy life (and for someone of Derek's personality that is more than likely), then the signs are that after the end of August 1993 he was being beaten by his illnesses.

Until then at least he continued to write and he was still capable of creative endeavour and cultural counter-attack. A spectacular example of the latter came in April 1993 when Bart's Hospital was threatened with closure by an insensitive health secretary in the Cabinet of an intransigent Conservative government driven not by a concern for improving the lives of people but by pure ideology. Derek wrote a letter of protest to the *Independent*, which to its credit the newspaper printed on its front page. He pointed out that Bart's was the world's oldest hospital, founded in the eleventh century by the monk Rahere in response to a dream about the saint. Derek emphasized how much he, as a patient, needed the tranquil pleasures of the eighteenth-century courtyard with its pavilion and fountain. Against the government he used Wittgenstein's thinking: 'Where an ideology has taken over, I see no doubt, and, since through doubt comes insight, a certain blindness.'[2] Derek also warned of the dangers of national amnesia: 'without our past our future cannot be reflected'. By virtue of its persuasiveness Derek's letter formed an important part of a widespread protest that led to the abandonment of the plans for the hospital's closure.

Sitting in his hospital bed on Wednesday, 19 August 1992, Derek wrote in his diary, 'I decided to make Blue w/out images – they hinder the imagination and beg a narrative and suffocate with arbitrary charm'.[3] But he had been deliberating about whether to use images or not in this film since 1987, so the decision was not a response to declining physical powers.[4] It was an aesthetic choice.

One thing that this decision ensured was that his final film could not be reviewed by critics along lines that had become recurrent in reviews of his work, whereby critical reservations about some aspects (script, actors' delivery, use of anachronism, overt sexuality) were in the end blanketed by approval of the sheer appearance of the film; in other words, beautiful and loving photography and visual design could not become the passport to critical approval. *Blue* has an entirely abstract image-track based on the colour International Klein Blue. The film therefore succeeds or fails on the combination of this with its very full and non-abstract sound track, based in the predicaments of being terminally ill. Upon completion, it was hailed by its maker: 'this is the first feature [film] to embrace the intellectual imperative of abstraction, it's moody, funny and distressing; it takes film to the boundary of the known world . . . The film is dedicated to HB and all true lovers' (2 March 1993).[5] The film is a plangent lament for a generation cut down by AIDS, and a representation of the predicaments and thoughts of an individual confronting his own treatment and mortality. It is also a film of yearning, focusing that feeling on colour, which is seen, as Yves Klein expressed it, as 'the universal love in which Man bathes'.[6] Since 1993 *Blue* has become the best thought of among all Derek's films. It received standing ovations from audiences at the Edinburgh and Venice film festivals, and contributed no doubt to the award to Derek in Germany in September 1993 of the first Rainer-Werner Fassbinder prize for 'extraordinary artistic oeuvre'.[7] The prize money this brought freed Derek from financial anxiety: from the anxiety of how, unable to work, he was going to pay for his last five months of mortal illness.

Since I wish to assert that the entire soundtrack of *Blue* (including sound-effects and apparent prose passages) amounts to a poem, we need to draw back at this stage, the better to set this claim in context. It is at least arguable that the central activity of Derek's creative life was poetry. But what is the evidence for this?

Some poems included in Derek's collection of poetry, *A Finger in the Fishes Mouth* (1972) are dated by their titles to 1964. From the mid-1970s the 'John Dee' script contains the poetry that made its way into the Elizabethan scenes of *Jubilee* (1978). In working on *The Tempest*, *The Angelic Conversation* and *Edward II* he was working with the poetry of others, and he showed extraordinary skill in cutting the poetry of pop songs to image-tracks in his pop promos; achieving something similar for classical music in the film for *Aria*. Beginning with *Dancing Ledge* (1984) all of his prose memoirs include his own poetry, including the final diary, *Smiling in Slow Motion*, which contains a devastating meditation on having AIDS, 'As the Clock Ticks'. I have already argued that the words in the black series of paintings can be related to the verbal–spatial spread and contextual sensitivity of concrete poetry. The notebooks for the film *The Last of England* label, in Derek's own hand, the words of the voice-overs as 'Poetry' and in *Smiling in Slow Motion* he says of the film *The Garden* that it 'has poems, a poetic narrative'.[8] In *Kicking the Pricks* he had explained *The Last of England* in similar terms: '[the film] works with image and sound, a language that is nearer to poetry than prose' (pp. 185–7).[9] To Simon Field in an interview he had asserted that '*The Angelic Conversation* is not narrative, it's poetry.'

Such claims can be examined by taking the Emperor Hirohito voice-over from *The Last of England* as an example. It begins: 'The sad old emperor bent beneath his black top hat smiles in the deathly sunlit silence.' Immediately we notice a subtle music arising from the alliteration of 's' (seven times) and 'b' (three times in four words) and assonance of 'a' (sad black hat) and 'i' (smiles silence). These devices contribute to underline an imagery that is simultaneously melancholy and sinister. The voice-over continues in octosyllabics:

The lady next door to me says
THERE HE IS! THERE'S HIROHITO
AND HIS EMPRESS NAGASAKE
Look! Johnny look! They're playing the
Funeral March for the Royal
Doulton. He stole the patterns way
back when you were a little boy . . .

And throughout this passage we hear a sad strain of music based on repetition of similar vowel sounds in the words 'lady, next, says, there, there, empress, playing, way, when'.

Without labouring the point too much it is possible to take one more example:

> Us kiddies weaned on food parcels
> From Uncle Randy in the wild west
> Choc-full o' comix and bubble gum
> . . .
> The bomb dropped with regular monotony
> Leaving us waiting – the frosty heart of
> England blighted each spring leaf
>   All aspiration withered in the blood.

The rhythms here include alliteration of 'k' (kiddies, uncle, comix), 'f' (food, from, full) and 'b' (bomb, blighted, blood). Alliteration cuts across the syntagmatic chain to enhance relationships, and as the words are selected and isolated here we can see how Derek's alliterations subtly reinforce the meaning and feeling in the words. There is also assonance of 'i' (four times) and of 'o' (nine times).

A play on words emerges. 'wild west/ choc-full o' comix and bubble gum' features light-hearted play with conventional spellings (choc for chock, o' for of, comix for comics) which would certainly not have been permitted at a 1950s prep school (off to which 'us kiddies' would have been packed, outside the holidays).[10] Is it my imagination, or do the phrases ('wild west'; 'choc-full o' comix'; 'bubble gum') convey a feeling of chewing? A less cheery play on words emerges in 'leaving . . . leaf' stretching across two lines of baleful meaning. The assonance of 'o' changes radically from the eating passage (choc, o', comix) to the gloomy 'The bomb dropped with regular monotony'. The phrase 'regular monotony' might seem redundant in meaning (a tautology) but instead the rhythm of the words, working together with three 'o' sounds in a row, enacts the meaning of the phrase. All the effects specified here subtly or subliminally emphasize and ramify the meanings of the poems. A final point to make concerns rhythm: the most memorable lines in the film possess strength not least as a result of being constituted from a subtle mix of trochee, iamb, spondee:

On every green hill mourners stand
And weep for the last of England

To return to *Blue*: parts of the soundtrack qualify as obviously poetic. The section at the end that begins 'Pearl fishers / In azure seas' deserves to be included in every anthology of modern poetry in English. It is great and memorable poetry of loss, mourning, grieving, mutability, love and the persistence of art. It and other sections are typeset as poems in the book published to accompany the film.[11] Such sections can thus be taken as poetry without having to labour the point. They are interspersed with passages that seem conversational, anecdotal and personal, mostly dealing with Derek's experience of attending hospitals, and which in the book are typeset as if they were prose. Yet the context of one of the obviously poetic passages suffices to show that the entire soundtrack deserves to be conceived as a poem.

In the pandemonium of image
I present you with the universal Blue
Blue an open door to soul
An infinite possibility
Becoming tangible

These lines are immediately followed by two sentences that as read in Nigel Terry's exasperated dry delivery produce a comic effect, not least through the very down-to-earth character that contrasts with the elevated thoughts and diction of the preceding lines: 'Here I am again in the waiting room. Hell on earth is a waiting room.' Yet the separation of parts of the sound track into poetry or prose will not hold up as soon as we realize that the lines above, apparently so prosaic, form a decasyllabic followed by an octo-syllabic in which the structure is consistent: both sentences begin with trochaic metre that flips over to iambic through the extra unstressed syllable formed by the article (definite and indefinite).

Poetry set as if it were great paragraphs of prose is a feature of the work of one of Derek's favourite poets, Allen Ginsberg. It will be objected that sound effects (bicycle bells, washing machine and fridge defrosting) are not poetry at all, but in defence it can be asserted that sound poetry has been a feature of modern poetry in various languages at least since the Futurist poets.

On Christmas Eve 1993 Derek wrote in his diary, 'Meanwhile life ticks to a close, thank God. I really am a little fed up . . .'.[12] Some time in the nineteen days left to him after his 52nd birthday, he told Collins that he was starving himself to death.[13] He died on 19 February 1994.

One thing certain about Derek Jarman the man is that he lived life fully, ducking no challenges, following no quietist paths, but finding and making opportunities for himself, not content to take the back seat of 'art films' but insisting on making feature films for as wide a general release as could be coaxed or cajoled out of a confused distribution system. His legacy to us is a legacy of art: his films, his paintings, his writings including his poetry, his garden at Prospect Cottage. All these activities came to have a more or less collaborative nature, including his last series of paintings as he applied the paint together with an assistant, Piers Clemmet or Karl Lydon.

The art critic of the *New York Times* recently (February 2010) expressed dissatisfaction with the character of the art that has been on show in recent years:

The goal in . . . being an artist should be individuation and difference, finding a voice of your own. Instead, we're getting example after example of . . . takes on that . . . early '70s mix of Conceptual, Process, Performance, installations and language-based art . . . most associated with the label post-minimalism . . .

[W]e've come to understand that dominant styles like Abstract Expressionism, Minimalism and Pop art are at best gross simplifications of their periods . . .

What's missing is art that seems made by one person out of intense personal necessity, often by hand.

Derek navigated through this intellectual terrain years ago: in the section on art school and individualism in *Kicking the Pricks* (1987) he reflected on his education in the late 1950s and early 1960s:

The next thing I learnt was that I had to become an individual, to individuate, to become myself; you can only do this alone; I was doing this quietly and quite well even at eighteen. Then I went to The Slade, where I joined up with millions of the fuckers who were being taught to become themselves; I joined the crowd, it was crowded being an individual.[14]

The paradox so clearly set out here all hinges around the contradiction between 'you can only do this alone' and 'fuckers who were being taught to become themselves'. In his rejection of big movements such as Pop ('the air-conditioned nightmare of Pop')[15] he stubbornly stuck to an individual's path. In painting this led exactly to 'art that seems made by one person out of intense personal necessity and by hand' in Derek's entire output from the GBH series to the end of his life.

Film, by contrast, depends on its collaborations for its very existence, and in this area Derek moved instinctively away from the feature-film convention of overbearing director being deified

and addressed as 'sir' on set. In an interview from 1986 about
Caravaggio in *Square Peg* he referred to the problem of conventional
feature-film production being 'painful work': 'it's up to film directors
to alter this and I really tried to do this both with *The Tempest*
and this film . . . I think it's terribly important to restore that kind
of William Morris philosophy'.[16] He explains that philosophy as
involving a belief that everything that has survived comes invested
with all the thoughts people had about it during the process of
making. Derek's own practice in this respect reflected his belief that
artists need to redefine themselves as artists and spread creativity
around, first voiced in *Jubilee*. The result of his way of working was
the creation of a sort of mobile craft workshop (the people with
whom he worked on his films).[17] Tilda Swinton has characterized
his way of working as 'pre-industrial'[18] thereby equating the conventional studio feature film and the industrial (that is, opposed
to craft). Derek could not have been educated in art when he
was (especially under Robin Noscoe) without taking in a line
of descent from Walter Pater to William Morris, Eric Gill and
Nikolaus Pevsner. Pevsner had taught Derek at King's College
and his book about the Modern Movement in architecture linked
William Morris and the Bauhaus; while as we have seen Noscoe
emblazoned a quotation from Eric Gill on the Canford school art
hut. Derek emerges as a triumphant exemplar of craft production
in the post-modern post-Frankfurt School post-Morris field in
which 'an ideologically-motivated approach to the making of things'
comes to the forefront.[19] As Derek put it, 'After all, if work is not a
joy, is it really worth it?' and towards the end of his life he reiterated
that film-making should be fun, and the process an end in itself.[20]

For Morris creative work was the goal, and he rejected other
forms of work as mere means to an end. 'What business have
we with art', he wrote in 1883, 'unless we can all share it?' Morris
believed that beauty gives pleasure; that objects should be beautiful;
that work, being a necessity, should give pleasure; that all work done

with pleasure amounts to art. Pleasure therefore is constituted from a sensory phenomenon, but also becomes a moral imperative. According to Norman Kelvin, 'Paterian equation of aesthetic experience with pleasure, even happiness, remain[s] at the root of Post-Modernism.'[21] In accepting all these precepts, and in forcing the varied fields he worked in to yield to his demands that he should be able to work in those fields according to those precepts, Derek forged an ethics out of his aesthetics.

References

Preface

1 'Hugely charismatic,' Ruth Rosenthal, interview with the author, 18 July 2009; 'charismatic', Tilda Swinton, *400 Blows* interview; 'very charming', Tony Peake, interview with the author, 29 July 2009; 'charismatic', Andrew Logan, interview with the author 10 August 2009; 'everyone who met Derek thought he was their best friend', John Maybury, video interview on DVD of *Jubilee*.

1 The View from Dungeness

1 Derek Jarman, radio interview with Antony Clare, published in Clare, *In the Psychiatrist's Chair* (London, 1992), p. 182.
2 For instance, Robert MacFarlane, *The Wild Places* (London, 2007), p. 261.
3 Roger Deakin, *Notes from Walnut Tree Farm* (London, 2009), p. 74.
4 Derek Jarman, *Modern Nature: the Journals of Derek Jarman* (London, 1991), p. 30.
5 Jarman, *Kicking the Pricks* (London, 1996), p. 167, first published as *The Last of England* (London, 1987).
6 Christopher Lloyd, 'The Derek Jarman Garden Experience', in Roger Wollen, ed., *Derek Jarman: A Portrait* (London, 1996), pp. 147–52.

2 Schoolboy and Student

1 Derek Jarman, BBC Radio broadcast interview, transcript reprinted in Anthony Clare, *In the Psychiatrist's Chair* (London, 1992), pp. 168–9.

2 Adult diary quoted by Tony Peake, *Derek Jarman* (London, 1999), p. 23.

3 Derek Jarman, *Modern Nature: The Journals of Derek Jarman* (London, 1991), pp. 266–7.

4 Jarman, *Modern Nature*, p. 191.

5 Ibid., p. 7.

6 Ibid., p. 10.

7 Ibid.

8 Jarman, *Kicking the Pricks* (London, 1996), pp. 19–21.

9 Ibid., p. 197 and Jarman, *Modern Nature*, p. 143.

10 The amazing indictment is in John Le Carré, *A Murder of Quality: The Novel and Screenplay* (London, 1991). The novel was first published in 1962.

11 Jarman, *Kicking the Pricks*, p. 181.

12 Peake, *Derek Jarman*, p. 53 and note.

13 Keith Collins, conversation with the author, 30 July 2009.

14 Jarman, *Dancing Ledge* (London 1984), pp. 219–20.

15 Peake, *Derek Jarman*, p. 56.

16 Ibid., p. 77.

17 Jarman, video interview with Colin McCabe (British Film Institute, 1991).

18 Peake, *Derek Jarman*, pp. 94, 100.

19 Jarman, *Dancing Ledge*, p. 22.

20 Both quotations from Jarman, *Modern Nature*, p. 84.

3 Designing for Others, Painting, Super-8

1 All these are illustrated in Roger Wollen, ed., *Derek Jarman: A Portrait* (London, 1996), p. 92.

2 Tony Peake, *Derek Jarman* (London, 1999), p. 133.

3 Ibid., p. 138.

4 Seen by the author from the back of the family car returning from a holiday in Scotland.

5 This tendency in Jarman is emphasized by Andrew Logan, conversation with the author, 10 August 2009.

6 Peake, *Derek Jarman*, p. 161.

7 For example, a green coastal landscape in a private collection, and the yellow 'Untitled' painting reproduced in Wollen, *Derek Jarman: A Portrait*, p. 56.

8 Derek Jarman, *Dancing Ledge* (London, 1984), p. 75.

9 Ibid., p. 105.

10 Ibid., p. 95.

11 Ibid.

12 Ibid., pp. 122–3.

13 Ibid., p. 123.

14 John Russell Taylor, review of Jarman's exhibition at the ICA, *The Times*, 7 February 1984.

15 Sir Peter Maxwell-Davies, interview in Channel Four documentary 'Hell on Earth: the desecration and resurrection of *The Devils*' (2002).

16 John Baxter, *An Appalling Talent: Ken Russell* (London, 1973), p. 229.

17 Jarman, *Dancing Ledge*, p. 95.

18 Jarman, *Kicking the Pricks* (London, 1996), p. 235.

19 Jarman, *Dancing Ledge*, p. 28.

20 Jarman, *Kicking the Pricks*, p. 170.

21 Both quotations from Jarman, *Dancing Ledge*, p. 132.

22 Ibid., p. 131.

23 Typescript of 'An interview with Derek Jarman' by Clive Hodgson, about the 8-mm films 1970–76, n.d. Jarman gives the date of 'Electric Fairy' as 'about 1970'. British Film Institute (BFI) archives Derek Jarman II catalogue, Box 56. In an entry in a notebook ('The Jigsaw. Part II') dated 7 February 1983, Jarman dates 'Electric Fairy' to the autumn of 1970 (BFI Jarman II, Notebook 18).

24 Jarman, *Dancing Ledge*, p. 129.

25 Ibid., p. 124.

26 Both quotations ibid., p. 128.

27 Ibid., p. 134.

28 Ibid., p. 225–6.

29 Ibid., p. 134.

30 Ibid., p. 137.

31 Keith Collins, conversation with the author, 30 July 2009.

32 Steven Dillon, *Derek Jarman and Lyric Film: The Mirror and the Sea* (Austin, TX, 2004), pp. 34–49.

33 B. S. Johnson, *The Unfortunates* (London, 1969).

34 Jarman, *Dancing Ledge*, p. 65.

35 BFI archive, Derek Jarman Main listing, Box 3 Item 1b.

4 The Feature Films of the 1970s

1 In a way posited in René Girard's *La Violence et le sacré* (Paris, 1972). Among Derek's circle it is possible that Patrik Steede was aware of this book, but also possible that Dom Sylvester Houédard or Jack Welch had read it.

2 Steven Dillon places Sebastian as hero in *Derek Jarman and Lyric Film: the Mirror and the Sea* (Austin, TX, 2004), pp. 62–70. So does Michael O'Pray, *Derek Jarman: Dreams of England* (London, 1996), pp. 80–94. O'Pray's substantial commentary on *Sebastiane* overplays an 'end of Empire' interpretation (the Roman Empire lasted another century and a half after the date of the represented events *c.* AD 300) and underplays the question of the turnover of religions.

3 Derek Jarman, *At Your Own Risk: A Saint's Testament* (London, 1992), p. 83.

4 Jarman, *Dancing Ledge* (London, 1984), p. 142.

5 Rowland Wymer, *Derek Jarman* (Manchester, 2005), pp. 45–7.

6 Chris Lippard, telephone interview with Derek Jarman, November 1993, transcribed in Lippard, ed., *By Angels Driven: The Films of Derek Jarman* (Westport, CT, 1996), p. 166.

7 Jarman, *Dancing Ledge*, p. 142.

8 Christopher Hobbs, interview in the film *Jubilee: A Time Less Golden*, Spencer Leigh, 2003.

9 BFI Jarman Main, Box 3 Item 4c.

10 Jarman, *Dancing Ledge*, p. 179.

11 Jarman quoted in French publicity for *Jubilee*, BFI Jarman Main, Box 4 Item 11a.

12 It is neglected or misunderstood by Wymer, *Derek Jarman*; O'Pray, *Derek Jarman*; Tracy Biga and Lawrence Driscoll in Lippard,

By Angels Driven; and William Pencak, *The Films of Derek Jarman* (Jefferson, NC, 2002).

13 This dream occasioned Jarman's unrealized film project 'Akenaten'. See Jarman, *Up in the Air: Collected Film Scripts* (London, 1996), pp. 1–40.

14 Text of the T-shirt essay can be found on the Criterion Collection DVD release of *Jubilee* (2003).

15 Jarman, *Smiling in Slow Motion* (London 2000), p. 151, entry for Saturday, 20 June 1992.

16 Jarman, video interview with Colin McCabe (BFI, 1991).

17 Both reviews are quoted in BFI Jarman II, Box 56 Item 3.

18 See Herwarth Röttgen, *Il Caravaggio: Ricerche e Interpretazione* (Rome, 1974).

19 Tony Peake, *Derek Jarman* (London, 1999), p. 260–61, has sorted out what did happen.

20 Jarman, *Dancing Ledge*, p. 184.

21 Ibid., p. 185.

22 Nikolaus Pevsner and Alexandra Wedgwood, *The Buildings of England: Warwickshire* (Harmondsworth, 1966), p. 409.

23 O'Pray, *Derek Jarman*, p. 117.

24 Wymer, *Derek Jarman*, pp. 78–80, on the theme of death.

25 Jarman, *Kicking the Pricks*, p. 122.

26 Jarman, interview with Toby Rose, *Coaster* (1984) quoted in Peake, *Derek Jarman*, p. 549, n. 46.

5 Painting, Writing, Pop Promos

1 His passport of the time describes him as 'film director'.

2 Derek Jarman, interview in *Square Peg*, 1986, BFI Jarman II, Box 26 Item 7.

3 For Jarman's enthusiasm, see for example *Kicking the Pricks* (London, 1996), pp. 184–5.

4 Ken Butler, conversation with the author, 30 March 2010.

5 Jarman in 1984 and 1991, quoted in Tony Peake, *Derek Jarman* (London, 1999), p. 326.

6 Actually film of the fountain in the garden of Castle Howard, Yorkshire.

7 Jarman, *Dancing Ledge* (London, 1984), p. 215.

8 For instance, Jarman, *Kicking the Pricks*, pp. 89–90.

9 For instance, Alexander Walker quoted in Michael O'Pray, *Derek Jarman: Dreams of England* (London, 1996), p. 119.

10 Explained by Peake, *Derek Jarman*, pp. 264–5.

11 Thus giving gay men a role as vanguard of a much broader struggle. The idea of being out of step with social conventions and laws is, in literature, Byron's lesson. See J. J. McGann, 'Introduction' to *The Oxford Authors: Byron* (Oxford and New York, 1986). It was also Nerval's, Hugo's and Baudelaire's, Walter Pater's, Oscar Wilde's, Jaroslav Hasek's and Ford Madox Ford's lesson. For Ford see Arthur Mizener's 'Afterword' to Ford Madox Ford, *Some Do Not . . . & No More Parades* (New York, 1964). This is a succinct summary of the overall importance of the idea.

12 Derek read Keith Vaughan's journals in September 1989: Jarman, *Modern Nature: The Journals of Derek Jarman* (London, 1991), p. 153.

13 Both quotations from Jarman, *Kicking the Pricks*, p. 68.

14 'I was out every night, there was nothing to do during the daytime . . .', Jarman, *Kicking the Pricks*, p. 68.

15 Despite an interesting section on Jarman in Laurie Ede, *British Film Design: A History* (London, 2010), pp. 161–5, Ede reveals that she doesn't understand why Jarman would want to use anachronisms in his work.

16 Peake, *Derek Jarman*, p. 315.

17 Jarman, *Dancing Ledge*, p. 245.

18 Ibid., p. 229.

19 Ibid., p. 228.

20 Ibid., pp. 232–4.

21 Ibid., p. 128.

22 Ibid., p. 235.

23 Ibid., p. 244.

24 Ibid., pp. 246, 241.

25 Ibid., p. 246–9, 251.

26 Ibid., p. 249.

27 Ibid., p. 247.

28 Jarman, interview in *Performance Magazine* (February/March 1984), p. 19.

29 Derek's exhibition opened at the end of February; the first actions of the miners' strike occurred in the first half of March.

30 It is interesting, looking back over more than a quarter of a century, to see the company in which Jarman's films found themselves. Other events at the ICA that month included showing of Henry Jaglom's *Can She Bake a Cherry Pie?*, Monstrous Regiment's *Enslaved by Dreams* and Ken McMullen's *Ghost Dance*.

31 BFI Jarman II, Box 57 Item 5, undated and the publication, a gay magazine, unspecified.

32 Jarman, *Dancing Ledge*, p. 229 ('the technical drawings of Robert Fludd'), and p. 188. The two images of Fludd's I have named are from his *Utriusque Cosmi Maioris* (Oppenheim, 1617) and were more readily accessible in the early 1980s in Joscelyn Godwin, *Robert Fludd: Hermetic Philosopher and Surveyor of Two Worlds* (London, 1979).

33 William Blake, *Milton*, copy A, British Museum, London, plate 20 (text), 21 (image). Copies of *Milton* can be viewed online on the William Blake Archive website.

34 Jarman, *Kicking the Pricks*, p. 190.

6 8 Millimetre versus 35 Millimetre

1 Some of the filming for 'Depuis le Jour' was done by Chris Hughes. In *Kicking the Pricks* (London, 1966), Jarman uses the example of bluebells in Kentish woods to demonstrate the cumbersome inflexibility of 35 mm (p. 169).

2 See Jarman, *Kicking the Pricks*, pp. 92–109.

3 Jarman, *Dancing Ledge* (London, 1984), p. 128.

4 Video recording of interview with Jarman by Simon Field, Zeitgeist Video's release of *The Angelic Conversation* on DVD in the collection *Glitterbox* (2008).

5 James Mackay, conversation with the author, 8 March 2010.

6 Adam Mars-Jones, *New Statesman* (25 April 1986), p. 29.

7 Jarman, *Dancing Ledge*, p. 235. On *Caravaggio*, see also L. Bersani and U. Dutoit, *Caravaggio* (London, 1999).

8 Jarman, *Derek Jarman's Caravaggio: The Complete Film Script and Commentaries* (London, 1986), p. 25.

9 Jarman also claims Shakespeare as 'a supporter from the past', that is a supporter of gay causes: Simon Field interview.

10 Information in this paragraph comes from an audio tape of Jarman in a discussion at the BFI chaired by Derek Malcolm after preview screening of *Caravaggio*, 1986. The tape is included in the Zeitgeist Video DVD release of *Caravaggio* (2008).

11 On television, 12 March 1986, using the film director Alan Parker as mouthpiece: see Tony Peake, *Derek Jarman* (London, 1999), p. 358, and the rebuttal by David Robinson of Parker's shabby attempt to squash Jarman, in *The Times* (12 March 1986), BFI Jarman II, Caravaggio Box 7.

12 Nigel Pollitt, *City Limits* (24 April–1 May 1986), p. 23; Nigel Andrews, *Financial Times* (25 April 1986).

13 Lawrence Gowing, *Times Literary Supplement*, BFI Jarman II, Large Notebook 7.

14 Jarman, in *Square Peg*, 1986, BFI Jarman II, Box 26, Item 7.

15 Jarman, *Modern Nature: The Journals of Derek Jarman* (London, 1991), p. 28, and *At Your Own Risk: a Saint's Testament* (New York, 1993), p. 27.

16 Edward Behr, *Newsweek* (5 May 1986).

17 Dilys Powell, *Punch* (30 April 1986).

18 Undated interview with Martin Sutton, *Stills*, BFI Jarman II, Item 7.

19 'A. G-D' in *Harpers*, Alan Stanbrook in *Stills*, John Russell Taylor in *Sight and Sound*, and Iain Johnstone in *The Sunday Times*, all in BFI Jarman II, Item 7.

20 Mark Finch, *Monthly Film Bulletin* (April 1986), pp. 99–100.

21 *Sunday Telegraph* (27 April 1986).

22 David Robinson, in *The Times* (25 April 1986).

23 *Mail on Sunday* (27 April 1986).

24 On the constraints of 35 mm see Jarman, interview with Michael O'Pray in *Monthly Film Bulletin*, LIII/627 (April 1987).

25 Jarman interviewed in *Marxism Today* (October 1987).

26 Annette Kuhn estimates 150 cuts for one three-minute sequence, in *Family Secrets: Acts of Memory and Imagination* (London and New York, 1995), p. 110.

27 Jarman, *Kicking the Pricks*, pp. 185–7.

28 Nicholas Hytner, director's spoken commentary on the 2007 DVD release of *The History Boys*.

29 Tilda Swinton in U.S. National Public Radio interview, broadcast in Austin, Texas (1 July 2008).

30 Robert Hewison, *Future Tense: A New Art of the Nineties* (London, 1990), p. 75.

31 Michael O'Pray, *Derek Jarman: Dreams of England* (London, 1996), p. 156.

32 Kuhn, *Family Secrets*, pp. 119–20.

33 Gus Van Sant, *Even Cowgirls Get the Blues & My Own Private Idaho* (London and Boston, 1993), p. xxxiv.

34 Will Self, 'Birth of the Cool', *Guardian Weekend* (6 August 1994).

35 Some of this poetry is reproduced in *Kicking the Pricks* (typeset as prose) but this does not correspond exactly to what can be heard in the final film.

36 BFI Jarman II, The Last of England, Box 12, Item 13.

37 Jarman, *Kicking the Pricks*, p. 188.

38 BFI Jarman II, The Last of England, Box 12, Item 13.

39 BFI Jarman II, Notebook – The Last of England, Box 12, Item 12.

40 Jarman, *Kicking the Pricks*, p. 215.

41 Jarman, interview with Simon Field.

42 Jarman, *Kicking the Pricks*, p. 167.

7 1986 and After

1 Interview from 1987, quoted in Tony Peake, *Derek Jarman* (London, 1999), p. 360.

2 Geoffrey Robertson QC, 'The Mary Whitehouse Story', *The Times* (24 May 2008).

3 Mary Whitehouse, quoted in Simon Watney, *Policing Desire: Pornography, AIDS and the Media*, 2nd edn (Minneapolis, 1989), p. 121.

4 For this and other information in this chapter see Tony Peake, *Derek Jarman*, p. 357.

5 BFI Jarman II, Caravaggio, Box 7 contains a copy of the letter.

6 Reviews in the *Guardian* (28 October 1976) and the *Observer* (31 October 1976).

7 Incident recounted in Derek Jarman, *Kicking the Pricks* (London, 1996), p. 90.

8 Audio recording of audience discussion with Jarman chaired by Derek Malcolm after British Film Institute screening of *Caravaggio*

(1986) included in Zeitgeist Video's DVD release of *Caravaggio* in *Glitterbox* (2008).

9   Transcript in BFI Jarman II, Notebook 20.

10 BFI transcript; Peake, *Derek Jarman*, pp. 420–21.

11 Jarman, *Modern Nature: The Journals of Derek Jarman* (London, 1991), p. 265.

12 Ibid., p. 263

13 BFI Jarman II, Box 12 Item 12.

14 See Jarman, *Modern Nature*, p. 240.

15 Jarman, *Derek Jarman's Garden* (London, 1995) p. 67.

16 Jarman, *Modern Nature*, pp. 228, 239–40.

17 Jarman, *Smiling in Slow Motion* (London, 2000), p. 387.

18 There are particularly strong encomia of Collins throughout Jarman, *Smiling*.

19 BFI Jarman II, Item 17, Dancing Ledge diaries, p. 61.

20 BFI Jarman II, Item 22.

21 BFI Jarman II, Notebook 20, entry entitled 'Monday'.

22 Jarman, *Kicking the Pricks*, p. 225.

23 BFI Jarman Main, Box 4, Item 5.

24 Jarman mentions Finlay in *Modern Nature*, p. 25.

25 There were of course limits to post-Wolfenden freedoms, as Simon Watney expounds in *Policing Desire*, pp. 60–66.

26 Jarman, *Kicking the Pricks*, p. 82.

27 Jarman in Anthony Clare, *In the Psychiatrist's Chair* (London, 1992), p. 167.

28 BFI Jarman II, Notebook 20.

29 Jarman, 'A Serpent in the form of a £', *Art Monthly*, 114 (March 1988).

30 Peake's *Derek Jarman* contains good sections on these bills and their implications, pp. 464–6, 418–21.

31 Peake, *Derek Jarman*, p. 418.

32 Jarman, *Kicking the Pricks*, p. 62.

33 Stone's article appeared in *The Sunday Times* (10 January 1988); Jarman's reply in the same newspaper (17 January 1988).

34 BFI Jarman II, Item 4.

35 Jarman, interview in *Sounds* (11 February 1984).

36 I use the word intending the sense meant by scholars who discuss 'Outsider Art': art made by untrained artists. Jarman was not an

outsider, but his garden slightly resembles such outsider gardens.

37 'I have the head of Mausolus and a plaster foot', Jarman, *Derek Jarman's Caravaggio: The Complete Film Script and Commentaries* (London, 1986), p. 28.

38 Mostly taken for the book *Derek Jarman's Garden*.

39 Keith Collins, Preface to *Derek Jarman's Garden*.

40 Jarman, *Modern Nature*, p. 273.

41 Jarman, *Kicking the Pricks*, p. 175.

42 Jarman, *Modern Nature*, p. 56.

43 'Derek Jarman Late Works', 8 September – 13 October 2001, Metropole Galleries, Folkestone, Kent. Information about the state of the paintings from Kelvin Pawsey (who hung the paintings), conversation with the author, 7 August 2009.

44 The phrase 'great summers' is Oliver Rackham's: *Ancient Woodland: Its History, Vegetation and Uses in England*, new edn (Dalbeattie, 2003), p. 407.

45 Both quotations, 8 and 9 July 1991, from Jarman, *Smiling*, p. 32.

46 Ibid., p. 34.

47 Jarman, *War Requiem* (London, 1989), p. 35.

48 Jarman, *Modern Nature*, p. 171.

49 Ibid., pp. 198–204; see also pp. 140–41.

8 Filming Plays, Painting Words, Being Ill

1 Tony Peake, *Derek Jarman* (London, 1999), p. 397.

2 Madame Anne-Louise Germaine de Staël, *De l'Allemagne*, II, xv (Paris, 1810), translated by the author.

3 BFI Jarman II, Item 17, Dancing Ledge diaries, vol. 1 The Jigsaw. See also Derek Jarman, *Dancing Ledge* (New York, 1993), p. 186.

4 BFI Jarman II, Notebook 20, Borrowed Time, Book I: thus probably from 1987, at the height of his commitment to Super 8.

5 Peter Brook, *The Empty Space*, new edn (New York, 1996), p. 79.

6 Ibid., p. 78.

7 Ibid., pp. 66–7.

8 John Wyver, conversation with the author, 15 May 2010.

9 Frank Kermode, *Times Literary Supplement* (16 May 1980).

10 Jarman, *Smiling in Slow Motion* (London, 2000), p. 153.

11 Ibid., p. 303.

12 Ibid., p. 167.

13 Ibid., pp. 139, 140, 144.

14 See Jarman, Terry Eagleton and Colin McCabe, *Wittgenstein: The Terry Eagleton Script; The Derek Jarman Film* (London, 1993). For Trevor Griffiths, see Mike Poole and John Wyver, *Powerplays: Trevor Griffiths in Television* (London, 1984).

15 Ken Butler, conversation with the author, 31 March 2010. Ray Monk, *Ludwig Wittgenstein: The Duty of Genius* (New York, 1990).

16 Monk, *Ludwig Wittgenstein*, p. 262.

17 Jarman, interview with C. Lippard in Lippard, ed., *By Angels Driven: The Films of Derek Jarman* (Westport, CT, 1996), p. 165.

18 Jarman, *Chroma: A Book of Colour* (Woodstock, NY, 1995), pp. 137, 139.

19 Ludwig Wittgenstein, *Remarks on Colour* (Berkeley and Los Angeles, 1977), no. 60.

20 Monk, *Ludwig Wittgenstein*, p. 561.

21 Brook, *The Empty Space*, p. 60.

22 Jarman, interview with Simon Field.

23 Toyah Willcox gives a fulsome tribute to Jarman in an interview in Spencer Leigh's film, *Jubilee: A Time Less Golden* (2003) included in the Criterion Collection DVD of *Jubilee*.

24 See Sandy Powell's printed interview tribute in the booklet included in Zeitgeist Video's DVD *Glitterbox* (2008).

25 Information from Ken Butler, conversation with the author, 31 March 2010.

26 Information from Richard Salmon, conversation with the author, 12 March 2010.

27 Peake, *Derek Jarman*, p. 521.

28 'Ataxia which I call Wobble', p. 360, 'Mr Legless', p. 352, of Jarman, *Smiling*.

29 Ken Butler, 'All the Rage', essay reprinted from *Vogue* in the catalogue of the *Evil Queen* exhibition (Manchester, 1994), quoting Jarman, pp. 12–14.

30 Andrew Logan, conversation with the author, 10 August 2009.

31 Butler, 'All the Rage', p. 22.

9 In the End, the Poet

1   Jarman, *Smiling in Slow Motion* (London, 2000), p. 269.
2   The letter is reproduced in Jarman, *Smiling*, pp. 338–9.
3   Ibid., p. 198.
4   See BFI Jarman II, Notebook 20 'MNEMOSYNE. Borrowed Time July 1987'.
5   Jarman, *Smiling*, p. 320.
6   Yves Klein quoted by Jarman, BFI Jarman II, Box 16 'International Blue', March 1988.
7   Tony Peake, *Derek Jarman* (London, 1999), p. 527.
8   BFI Jarman II, Item 13, Last of England Notebook II; *Smiling*, p. 203.
9   Jarman, *Kicking the Pricks* (London, 1996), pp. 185–7.
10 The spellings of these words (which form part of the film) are taken from a version of the Emperor Hirohito voice-over printed in Jarman, *Kicking the Pricks*, p. 179 (typeset there as prose).
11 *Blue: Text of a Film by Derek Jarman* (London, 1993), pp. 28–30.
12 Jarman, *Smiling*, p. 385.
13 Peake, *Derek Jarman*, p. 532.
14 Jarman, *Kicking the Pricks*, p. 75.
15 Jarman, *Dancing Ledge* (New York, 1993), p. 122.
16 BFI Jarman II, Item 7, Caravaggio box.
17 Don Boyd, the producer, pays tribute to this in his 'Introduction' to Jarman, *War Requiem* (London, 1989), pp. vii–x.
18 Tilda Swinton, interview on U.S. National Public Radio, broadcast Austin, Texas (1 July 2008).
19 See, for example, the essays by Norman Kelvin and Paul Greenhalgh in Linda Parry, ed., *William Morris* (New York, 1996), catalogue of the *William Morris 1834–1896* exhibition at the Victoria and Albert Museum, London. The quotation is from Paul Greenhalgh's essay in that catalogue, 'Morris after Morris', p. 366.
20 Jarman, *War Requiem*, p. 29, and interview from November 1993 in C. Lippard, ed., *By Angels Driven: The Films of Derek Jarman* (Westport, CT, 1996), p. 166.
21 Norman Kelvin, 'The Morris Who Reads Us', in Parry, ed., *William Morris*, p. 349.

Select Bibliography

This bibliography consists of sources I consulted in order to write this book, except for Ellis's and Stoschek's books which had not then appeared. It does not represent a comprehensive Derek Jarman bibliography. For that (before 1999) I refer the reader to Tony Peake's *Derek Jarman*. An essential part of research was accomplished by visits to Prospect Cottage, Dungeness, in 1989, 1990, 2009 and 2010.

Unpublished material

On-camera interview, Derek Jarman and Simon Field, included, dated 1989, in Zeitgeist Video DVD of *The Angelic Conversation* in *Glitterbox* (2008)

On-camera interview, Derek Jarman and Colin McCabe (British Film Institute, 1991)

On-camera interviews of Christopher Hobbs, Tilda Swinton, Simon Fisher Turner, Gaye Temple, on the *400 Blows* website

On-camera interviews of Toyah Willcox, Christopher Hobbs, Lee Drysdale, John Maybury, in *Jubilee: A Time Less Golden* (film by Spencer Leigh, 2003) in the Criterion Collection DVD of *Jubilee* (2003)

On-camera interviews of Nigel Terry, Derek Jarman, Karl Johnson, Tariq Ali, James Mackay; and *The Clearing* (Alex Bistikas, 1994), a short film featuring Derek Jarman, in the Zeitgeist Video DVD, *Glitterbox* (2008)

Conversations I had with Ruth Rosenthal, Clare Paterson, John Wyver, Andrew Logan, Tony Peake, Keith Collins, Richard Salmon, James Mackay, Kate Sorzana, Andrew Wilson, in 2009 and 2010

British Film Institute, archive of Derek Jarman's papers, at the time
   of my visit arranged into two catalogues, the Derek Jarman Main
   Catalogue and the Derek Jarman II Catalogue. My references follow
   this arrangement

Published articles and books

Baxter, John, *An Appalling Talent: Ken Russell* (London, 1973)

Bersani, L., and U. Dutoit, *Caravaggio* (London, 1999)

Blake, William, *Milton* (Boulder, CO, and New York, 1978)

Brook, Peter, *The Empty Space* (New York, 1996 [1968])

Byron, George Gordon, *The Oxford Authors: Byron*, ed. J. J. McGann
   (Oxford and New York, 1986)

Clare, Anthony, *In the Psychiatrist's Chair* (London, 1992)

Deakin, Roger, *Notes from Walnut Tree Farm* (London, 2008)

Dillon, Steven, *Derek Jarman and Lyric Film: The Mirror and the Sea*
   (Austin, TX, 2004)

Ede, Laurie, *British Film Design: A History* (London, 2010)

Ellis, Jim, *Derek Jarman's Angelic Conversations* (London, 2009)

Ford, Ford Madox, *Some Do Not . . . & No More Parades*, Afterword by
   Arthur Mizener (New York, 1964)

Ginsberg, Allen, *Howl and Other Poems* (San Francisco, 1956)

Girard, René, *La Violence et le sacré* (Paris, 1972)

Godwin, Joscelyn, *Robert Fludd: Hermetic Philosopher and Surveyor of Two
   Worlds* (London, 1979)

Hewison, Robert, *Future Tense: a new Art of the Nineties* (London, 1990)

Jarman, Derek, *A Finger in the Fishes Mouth* (Bettiscombe Press, Dorset: 1972)

——, 'A Serpent in the form of a £', *Art Monthly*, 114 (March 1988)

——, *At Your Own Risk: A Saint's Testament*, ed. Michael Christie (New
   York, 1993)

——, *Blue: Text of a Film by Derek Jarman* (London, 1993)

——, *Chroma: A Book of Colour* (New York, 1995)

——, *Dancing Ledge*, ed. Shaun Allen (New York, 1993 [1984])

——, *Derek Jarman's 'Caravaggio': The Complete Film Script and
   Commentaries* (London, 1986)

——, *Derek Jarman's Garden* (London, 1995)

——, *Evil Queen: The Last Paintings* (Manchester, 1994)

——, *Kicking the Pricks* (London, 1996) First published as *The Last of England* (London, 1987)

——, *Modern Nature: The Journals of Derek Jarman* (London, 1991)

——, *Queer* (Manchester, 1992)

——, *Queer Edward II* (London, 1991)

——, *Smiling in Slow Motion*, ed. Keith Collins (London, 2000)

——, *Up in the Air: Collected Film Scripts* (London, 1996)

——, *War Requiem* (London, 1989)

——, Terry Eagleton and Colin McCabe, *Wittgenstein: The Terry Eagleton Script, the Derek Jarman Film* (London, 1993)

Kuhn, Annette, *Family Secrets: Acts of Memory and Imagination* (London and New York, 1995)

Le Carré, John, *A Murder of Quality: The Novel and Screenplay* (London, 1991)

Lippard, Chris, ed., *By Angels Driven: The Films of Derek Jarman* (Westport, CT, 1996)

MacFarlane, Robert, *The Wild Places* (London, 2007)

Marlowe, Christopher, *Edward II* (1592) in *The Complete Plays* (London, 1999)

Moore, G. E., 'Wittgenstein's Lectures in 1930–33', in *Aesthetics*, ed. Harold Osborne (Oxford, 1972)

Monk, Ray, *Ludwig Wittgenstein: The Duty of Genius* (New York, 1990)

O'Pray, Michael, *Derek Jarman: Dreams of England* (London, 1996)

Parry, Linda, ed., *William Morris* (New York, 1996)

Peake, Tony, *Derek Jarman* (London, 1999)

Pencak, William, *The Films of Derek Jarman* (Jefferson, NC, 2002)

Pevsner, Nikolaus, and Alexandra Wedgwood, *The Buildings of England: Warwickshire* (Harmondsworth, 1966)

Poole, Mike and John Wyver, *Powerplays: Trevor Griffiths in Television* (London, 1984)

Rackham, Oliver, *Ancient Woodland, Its History, Vegetation and Uses in England*, new edn (Dalbeattie, 2003)

Röttgen, Herwarth, *Il Caravaggio: Ricerche e Interpretazione* (Rome, 1974)

Shakespeare, William, *The Tempest* (Shakespeare in Production), ed. Christine Dymkowski (Cambridge, 2000)

Staël, Anne-Louise Germaine de, *De l'Allemagne* (Paris, 1810)

Stoschek, Julia, et al., *Derek Jarman Super 8* (Cologne, 2010)

Van Sant, Gus, *Even Cowgirls Get the Blues & My Own Private Idaho* (London and Boston, 1993)

Vaughan, Keith, *Journals 1939–1977* (London, 1989)

Watney, Simon, *Policing Desire: Pornography, AIDS and the Media* (2nd edn, Minneapolis, MN, 1989)

Watney, Simon and Erica Carter, eds, *Taking Liberties* (London, 1989)

Wittgenstein, Ludwig, *Remarks on Colour* (Berkeley and Los Angeles, CA, 1977)

Wollen, Roger, ed., *Derek Jarman: A Portrait* (London, 1996)

Wymer, Rowland, *Derek Jarman* (Manchester, 2005)

Acknowledgements

Many thanks for the kindness and help given to me by Keith Collins. Thanks to James Mackay for being extremely helpful, especially in explaining the Super-8 films. Kind help also came from Kate Sorzana, Ruth Rosenthal, Clare Paterson, Andrew Logan, Vic Allan of the Dean Clough Galleries in Halifax, Richard Salmon, Andrew Wilson of Tate Britain, Ken Butler, Marya Spont, Sally Penfold and Kelvin Pawsey.

The quotations from Derek Jarman's writings, including the poems on pp. 52–3, and the paintings and drawings, are reproduced by kind permission of the Derek Jarman Estate.

Tony Peake deserves thanks for being unfailingly helpful, and also for having written his biography, *Derek Jarman* (London, 1999), without which my own book would simply not have been possible.

Thanks to John Wyver of Illuminations Television for, as he put it, 'giving [me] a bed for the night, feeding [me] and doing most of [my] research'! Sally Dinsmore and Jenny Webb facilitated my interest in Jarman and his work; Tania String, then of the University of Bristol, provided me with a forum for furthering it and encouraged me to use that opportunity.

I would like to thank the Dean of the College of Fine Arts, University of Texas at Austin, and John Yancey, the Chair of the Department of Art and Art History, for the grant of research leave that enabled me to undertake the research that contributed to this book. The Houston Endowment, and The Kimbell Art Foundation of Fort Worth provided material support for travel and research activities and my thanks go to them and to my colleague Professor Jeffrey Chipps Smith.

Photo Acknowledgements

The author and publishers wish to express their thanks to the below sources of illustrative material and / or permission to reproduce it.

Arts Council Collection: p. 156; photos author: pp. 12, 13, 15, 29, 96, 137, 138, 142, 143; photos The British Film Institute (BFI): pp. 34, 35, 41, 43, 75, 95, 112; photo courtesy of The Huntington Library, Art Collections, and Botanical Gardens, San Marino, CA: p. 100; Estate of Derek Jarman: p. 89; reproduced courtesy of the Derek Jarman Estate: pp. 6, 29, 34, 35, 41, 43, 47, 57, 66, 75, 89, 95, 96, 104, 107, 112, 116, 142, 145, 153, 156, 163, 166, 170; reproduced courtesy of Richard Salmon: p. 89; private collections: pp. 29, 95, 96; Tate, London /Art Resource: pp. 166, 170.